THE
PASSION
AND THE
EMPTY TOMB

JOHN ANKERBERG
&JOHN WELDON

HARVEST HOUSE PUBLISHERS

EUGENE, OREGON

Cover by Terry Dugan Design, Minneapolis, Minnesota

Cover image © thislife pictures/Alamy

THE PASSION AND THE EMPTY TOMB

Copyright © 2005 by John Ankerberg and John Weldon
Published by Harvest House Publishers
Eugene, Oregon 97402

Ankerberg, John, 1945–
  The Passion and the empty tomb / John Ankerberg, John Weldon.
      p. cm.
  Includes bibliographical references and indexes.
  ISBN 0-7369-1441-2 (pbk.)
  1. Jesus Christ—Resurrection. I. Weldon, John. II. Title.
  BT482.A55 2005
  232.9'7—dc22   2004024316

Printed in the United States of America

05 06 07 08 09 10 11 12 / VP-CF / 10 9 8 7 6 5 4 3 2 1

For the One who promised all people,
"I am the resurrection and the life.
He who believes in me will live, even though he dies;
and whoever lives and believes in me
will never die.
Do you believe this?"

JOHN 11:25-26

A Note from Author John Weldon

These words are written, and this book concluded, on June 11, 2004, the National Day of Mourning for Ronald Wilson Reagan, fortieth president of the United States—one of the greatest of all time and, as his life reveals, as American a figure as there will ever be. The timing of the words we write are so appropriate primarily because of Reagan's simple faith in Jesus Christ. When the world said goodbye to the former president for the last time—as he was laid to rest amid a glowing sunset over the vast blue Pacific—it had no hope at all of seeing him again. It was quite literally an eternal goodbye. But we who are believers knew we would see him again, not only shortly—but forever.

Christians do not "grieve like the rest of men, who have no hope" (1 Thessalonians 4:13) precisely *because* of the resurrection of Christ—and President Reagan's faith in the resurrection of his Lord is proof he still lives, and is now with his risen Savior.

CONTENTS

WHAT NEXT?

❧

THE PASSION OF THE CHRIST and the resurrection of the Christ are part of the same divine fabric. How each one of us allows ourselves to be knit into this fabric determines whether our future will be eternally wonderful or unendingly tragic. Mel Gibson's landmark film, *The Passion of the Christ,* though it has had an impact like no other, is at best a prequel to an event yet more compelling—something without which no life lived has meaning.

The 100 million or so people who have seen the power of *The Passion* in theaters need also to personally understand the power of the resurrection in their lives and make a decision about it, for it alone defines the quality of their lives forever.

After seeing Gibson's epic, a Zen Buddhist—whose religion characteristically views the universe as senseless and useless—commented,

> There's this girl I know, and she's a Christian...she has a beauty that's entirely different from anything I've ever seen, and it seems like her beauty and what she believes are all wrapped up together. And that makes me want to be a better person. And this movie, and the way Jesus chose to go through all of that, it makes

me want to be a better person. It's connected
somehow. It's different from anything else I know. I
just don't know what I'm supposed to do next....[1]

What a person does next is what this book, *The Passion and
the Empty Tomb*, is all about. We can know what we are to do
if we understand that, after Christ's passion, the resurrection
actually happened—and that Jesus "was declared with power
to be the Son of God by his resurrection from the dead"
(Romans 1:4).

If we understand this, there's only one proper response—to
turn from our sins and our own self which wear us out; to joy-
ously receive the eternal life to which we are called; to bow
before the only One in history to be raised from the dead as
proof of His deity; and to gladly acknowledge His claims over our
life. In other words, to personally accept the incarnation, the
atonement, and the resurrection in order to inherit eternal life as
the utterly free and gracious gift that it is. To trust Christ and
follow Him as closely as we can will be to learn our true purpose
in life, with all the pleasures and delights waiting now and in
eternity—joys that are secure regardless of what life may bring.

Those of us who are believers can also know what to do.
Many of us are not yet fully acquainted with the historical and
other evidence for Christ's resurrection. Becoming acquainted
with this can powerfully affect our commitment to the Christian life, including our level of devotion, sense of joy, conviction of truth, power in evangelism, perseverance in trial, and
overall trust in God. In their lasting influence and coming
rewards, these matters can in turn powerfully impact our
delights now and in eternity—all the wonderful things provided through God's love.

That's really what we do after the passion: inherit the love.
The resurrection is as much about the love of God as it is
about His passion—with the added element of joy. Pure joy.

1

THE FIRST ACT OF
AN ETERNAL DRAMA

❧

I was stunned....I was deeply, deeply moved. I left the theater in a stunned silence and drove home in a stupor....I've never been more moved by a piece of art.

I never thought this movie was going to affect me like this....I could not even muster a smile or a nod when passing people, like I normally do, while leaving the theater. I just sat, in the cold, in my car for a bit before I could drive home.

I am Pagan, also. And, no matter what, I am moved, and I was in shock when that movie was over.

REACTIONS TO *THE PASSION OF THE CHRIST*[1]

MEL GIBSON'S *The Passion of the Christ* is a movie of unequalled power not only because it so forcefully displays our sin and God's unending wrath against it, but because it offers a glimpse of what infinite love really is and does.

According to Gibson himself, the idea and the movie itself were both a divine undertaking: "Gibson…hopes his film will be an evangelism tool….He tells reporters that God put it in his heart to get the story of Christ's crucifixion on screen. Speaking to Christians in Colorado last summer, Gibson said: 'The Holy Ghost was working through me on this film, and I was just directing traffic.'"[2]

The Influence of The Passion

In a media-saturated culture, no movie can be expected to have a lasting impact on anyone's life. But *The Passion of the Christ* apparently came closer than any. According to researcher George Barna, one in three Americans saw the movie, and almost half of those were not "born again." Yet just 11 weeks after the film opened,

> about 13 million adults changed some aspect of their typical religious behavior because of the movie and about 11 million people altered some pre-existing religious beliefs because of the content of that film. That's enormous influence….More than any other movie in recent years, *The Passion* focused people on the person and purpose of Jesus Christ. In a society that revolves on relativism, spiritual diversity, tolerance and independence, galvanizing such intense consideration of Jesus Christ is a major achievement in itself.[3]

The film powerfully affected millions, far more than any other movie in history, and in ways only God Himself fully understands. It piqued the curiosity of millions, and opened doors to tens of millions of conversations. The gospel of Christ's death for our sins was displayed about as powerfully as possible. (Having an estimated 100,000 people receive Christ and 500,000 share Christ as the result of a single film is phenomenal.[4]) And it left viewers little choice. As Gibson said, "Moviegoers will be forced to make a decision about Christ after they leave the theater." Whatever further research might reveal about the movie's impact, it's likely just the tip of the iceberg.

As Gibson suggested above, heaven may indeed have played a directing role. The movie powerfully impacted Jews, Christians, and Muslims globally, as well as many secularists. By means of patently false charges of anti-Semitism, the movie's fame was spread around the world, not only confronting Abraham's physical children with their Messiah in ways unthinkable before, but generating such publicity that Christ's atonement will, at some point, be presented to perhaps a *billion* people.[5]

Even in Saudi Arabia, Cuba, and other places where *The Passion* is banned, pirated CDs are "selling like hotcakes." According to several sources the movie made "history in the Arab world."[6] In Egypt, Qatar, Syria, Lebanon, Jordan, and the United Arab Emirates, the film actually broke box office tallies. The recently freed nations of Afghanistan and Iraq, and other Muslim nations like Oman, were also impacted. *Christianity Today* reported one missionary in the region as saying, "This film is generating so much interest in Jesus and the Scriptures....Every Christian we are talking to seems to have a story or two."[7]

In God's plan then, it seems that huge numbers of the adherents of the three great Western faiths—Christianity, Islam, and Judaism—not to mention equal numbers of adherents of the great Eastern and secular faiths—have been and will be compellingly introduced to God's love through the authority of the atonement. As the apostle Paul indicated, the world will never cease to be blessed in Abraham and his Seed:

The promises were spoken to Abraham and to his seed. The Scripture does not say "and to seeds," meaning many people, but "and to your seed," meaning one person, who is Christ (Galatians 3:16).[8]

I will be with you and will bless you. For to you and your descendants I will give all these lands and will confirm the oath I swore to your father Abraham. I will make your descendants as numerous as the stars in the sky and will give them all these lands, and through your offspring [seed] *all nations on earth will be blessed* (Genesis 26:3-4).

The Events That Have Made History

The last 12 hours of Jesus' life are the longest in history and perhaps in all eternity. Prophetic fulfillment is a key theme throughout these hours, reminding us that what happened, despite the horror, is actually part of God's loving and eternal plan. Else, as Jesus asked, "How then would the Scriptures be fulfilled that say it must happen in this way?...But this has all taken place that the writings of the prophets might be fulfilled" (Matthew 26:54,56; see John 18:9; 19:28,36-37).

The *Passion* film begins in the garden of Gethsemane, where Jesus resists Satan's temptations. He is betrayed by Judas, arrested, abandoned by His disciples, and taken to Jerusalem. There He is confronted by the Jewish leaders and condemned to death. He is questioned by Annas, a former high priest, and Caiaphas, Annas's son-in-law. Afterwards, He is tried by the Sanhedrin and found guilty of blasphemy by proclaiming Himself the Son of God. He is sentenced to death.

Since only the Romans are able to execute criminals, He is sent to Pontius Pilate at the Antonia Fortress. Brought before Pilate, who finds nothing wrong with Him, He is referred to Herod, who then returns Him to Pilate, who reluctantly offers the crowd the option of releasing either Barabbas, a criminal, or Jesus. The crowd chooses Jesus to be condemned, and He is given to Roman soldiers, whipped bloody, given the crown of thorns, and brought back to Pilate, who attempts once more to have Him released. Unsuccessful, the governor turns the King of the Jews over to be crucified. Jesus carries His cross through the streets of Jerusalem to Golgotha, where He is nailed to it and utters His final words, commending His spirit into the Father's hands. Powerful local and cosmic events and a brief glimpse of the resurrection end the film.[9]

But such a quick overview communicates little of the impact of the events, as the movie so powerfully demonstrates. The longer summary that now follows is taken from the Gospels, with descriptions of Jesus' condition supplied by medical doctors.

In the Garden of Gethsemane

In the Garden of Gethsemane, after fulfilling His incomparable and miraculous teaching ministry, Jesus recognizes all too well the nature of the torture He is about to endure. Even for Him, the realization is almost too much:

> He began to be deeply distressed and troubled. "My soul is overwhelmed with sorrow to the point of death" (Mark 14:33-34).

> "Father, everything is possible for you. Take this cup from me. Yet not what I will, but what you will" (Mark 14:36).

The One who is God from all eternity is about to die the most torturous death imaginable. The strain of understanding what He is about to undergo is so huge that the capillaries in His forehead begin to break, His blood mixing with His perspiration:

"An angel from heaven appeared to him and strengthened him. And being in anguish [the Greek wording suggests the idea of engaging in combat], he prayed more earnestly, and his sweat was like drops of blood falling to the ground" (Luke 22:43-44). This condition, known as *hematidrosis*, is described in the medical literature, and it alone may have produced "marked weakness and shock."[10] And at this point the disciples themselves are "exhausted from sorrow" (verse 45).

Before the Jewish High Priest Caiaphas and the Sanhedrin

To those who come against Him in the Garden, Jesus observes, "This is your hour—when darkness reigns" (Luke 22:53). After His betrayal by Judas and arrest, all His disciples desert Him—not a single man supports Him in His bleakest hour. He is taken to the Jewish high priest, Caiaphas, and before the entire Sanhedrin—council of 71 elders—and the first of the illegal and fraudulent trials begins: "The chief priest and the Sanhedrin were looking for false evidence against Jesus so they could put him to death. But they did not find any, though many false witnesses came forward" (Matthew 26:59-60).

> It is God Himself being subjected to all this.... This is what makes, as Chesterton said, "dust and nonsense" of comparative religion.

The high priest himself charges Jesus under oath to declare whether or not He is the Messiah, the Son of God. "Yes, it is as you say," Jesus replied. "But I say to all of you: In the future you will see the Son of Man sitting at the right hand of the Mighty One and coming on the clouds of heaven" (verses 63-64). The apostle Luke records another statement of Jesus to the Sanhedrin: "But from now on, the Son of Man will be seated at the right hand of the mighty God" (Luke 22:69).

The response is predictable. Despite His innocence, Jesus is charged with blasphemy and therefore judged worthy of death according to Jewish law: "The high priest tore his clothes and said, 'He has spoken blasphemy! Why do we need any more witnesses? Look, now you have heard the blasphemy. What do you think?' 'He is worthy of death,' they answered" (Matthew 26:65-66).

At this point some of those present "spit in his face," mocked him, and cruelly "struck him with their fists" (verse 67). In addition, He was beaten by the guards. "They blindfolded him, struck him with their fists, and said, 'Prophesy!' And the guards took him and beat him" (Mark 14:64-65). In all likelihood, the beating was severe.

At the same time, the apostle Peter is unraveling. After forcefully promising Jesus he would never deny Him, even at the risk of death, and swearing it with an oath, Peter's triple denial of Jesus in the courtyard produces remorse and weeping so bitter that only he could describe it (Matthew 26:75).

Up to this early point, Jesus has endured hematidrosis and possible shock, an intensity of emotional agony and spiritual warfare we can scarcely imagine, betrayal by Judas, false arrest, abandonment by all His disciples, an illegal trial, condemnation to death, mockery, spitting, physical beatings, Peter's triple denial, and more. And it is God Himself being subjected to all this. Besides much else, this is what makes, as Chesterton said, "dust and nonsense" of comparative religion.

Before the Roman Governor Pontius Pilate and King Herod

Early in the morning Jesus is bound and led away to the Roman governor, Pontius Pilate—now "battered and bruised, dehydrated, and exhausted from a sleepless night."[11] Jesus' betrayer, Judas, recognizing his guilt in betraying an innocent man, returns his pay of 30 pieces of silver to the chief priests, leaves, and proceeds to commit suicide by hanging himself (Matthew 27:3-5). When Pilate learns Jesus is a Galilean and is under Herod's jurisdiction, he sends Him to that ruler, who happens to be in Jerusalem at the time. Herod asks Jesus many questions, but amazingly, Jesus does not respond to a single query. Herod and the soldiers then ridicule and mock Christ and return Him to Pilate. And previously enemies, that day Herod and Pilate become friends (Luke 23:6-12).

Jesus now stands before Pilate once more. He is silent again except for one critical answer. "You are a king, then!" exclaims Pilate. Jesus responds, "You are right in saying I am a king. In fact, for this reason I was born, and for this I came into the world, to testify to the truth. Everyone on the side of truth listens to me" (John 18:37).

The Roman governor is amazed that Jesus answers no other question. But he is also fearful of this man, and his fear proceeds to multiply. Pilate's wife sends him a terrifying message: "Don't have anything to do with that innocent man, for I have suffered a great deal today in a dream because of him" (Matthew 27:19).

Several times Pilate tells the furious crowd outside that Jesus is innocent and that he finds no basis for a death sentence (John 19:4-6). But the Jews insist, "We have a law, and according to that law he must die, because he claimed to be the Son of God." When Pilate hears this, he is even more afraid. He goes back inside the palace. "*Where do you come from?*' he asked Jesus, but Jesus gave him no answer" (verses 7-9).

While enduring what becomes six trials,[12] Jesus has been forced to walk some two-and-a-half miles back and forth in a grievously weakened condition. Yet all He has undergone is nothing compared to what is about to happen.

Flogging

Despite Pilate's recognition of Jesus' innocence, he gives in to the crowd. Knowing his own guilt, the governor attempts to cover his sin:

> When Pilate saw that he was getting nowhere, but that instead an uproar was starting, he took water and washed his hands in front of the crowd: "I'm innocent of this man's blood," he said. "It is your responsibility!" All the people answered, "Let his blood be on us and on our children!" Then he released Barabbas to them. But he had Jesus flogged, and handed him over to be crucified (Matthew 27:24-26).

"But he had Jesus flogged," hardly conveys what actually occurred. The Gospel accounts are so brief that the nature of what occurs is obscured. As Jesus is scourged, He is whipped full force by two soldiers (called lictors) on His shoulders, back, buttocks, and legs with heavy leather thongs containing balls or pieces of lead, bone, or other metal at the ends. While the Jews limited the number of lashes to 39 and apparently used normal whips, the Romans had no limits. They did as they pleased based on their mood and the circumstances. Jesus could actually have had twice the number mentioned—given the soldiers' hostile attitude toward Him. Further, the point of the flogging was to bring the prisoner close to collapse or death, and the Roman soldiers were experts here.

In the end, "the skin of the back is hanging in long ribbons and the entire area is an unrecognizable mass of torn, bleeding tissue and exposed bone. When it is determined by the centurion in charge that the prisoner is near death, the beating is finally stopped. The half-fainting Jesus is then untied and allowed to slump to the stone pavement, wet with His own blood."[13] "Pain and blood loss generally set the stage for circulatory shock,"[14] and not surprisingly, the length of survival on the cross usually coincided with the severity of the flogging.

The soldiers next mock the Lord, placing a scarlet robe on His blood-soaked body and a crown of thorns on His head—not just any thorns, but razor-sharp one-to-two-inch thorns that would dig deep into His scalp and produce copious bleeding. Worse, the previous condition of hematidrosis has made His skin particularly tender here.

> Unlike the traditional crown which is depicted by an open ring, the actual crown of thorns may have covered the entire scalp....The gospels state that the Roman soldiers continued to beat Jesus on the head. The blows would drive the thorns into the scalp (one of the most vascular areas of the body) and forehead, causing severe bleeding.[15]

Incredibly, they even pulled out chunks of His beard, as Isaiah prophesied 700 years earlier: "I offered my back to those who beat me, my cheeks to those who pulled out my beard; I did not hide my face from mocking and spitting" (Isaiah 50:6).

The scarlet color of blood and Jesus' robe are reminiscent of Isaiah 1:18: "Though your sins are like scarlet, they shall be as white as snow." The thorns bring another reminder: "Thorns first appeared after the fall, as a sign of the curse. Thus, the articles that He wore are symbols to show that Jesus took the sins (and the curse) of the world upon Himself."[16] The soldiers now rip off the scarlet robe. Since it is "adhered to the clots of blood and serum in the wounds, its removal causes excruciating pain just as in the careless removal of a surgical bandage, and almost as though He were again being whipped, the wounds once more begin to bleed. In deference to Jewish custom, the Romans return His garments."[17]

The Crucifixion

Now Jesus is forced to carry part of the 300-pound cross to the place of execution, the 75- to 125-pound patibulum, or crossbar.

> In spite of His efforts to walk erect, the weight of the heavy wooden beam, together with the shock produced by copious blood loss, is too much. He stumbles and falls. The rough wood of the beam gouges into the lacerated skin and muscles of the shoulders. He tries to rise, but human muscles have been pushed beyond their endurance.[18]

Simon the Cyrene is conscripted to carry it to Golgotha—a word that means "the Place of the Skull," supplying vivid imagery for a place of execution.

A large number of people have been following along to the place of crucifixion. The sight is so ghastly that they are weeping. Yet Jesus tells them not to weep for Him, but rather to weep for themselves and their children because of the judgment that is coming upon them (Luke 23:27-31)—a prophecy fulfilled by the Roman commander Titus when he mercilessly destroyed Jerusalem in the year 70.

The greatest drama in human history is about to begin—the death of Son of God at the hands of His own creatures. Here is an eternal wonder. And it is not just any death, but death by crucifixion, perfected into a vicious torture by the Romans and described by the famous Jewish historian Josephus as "the most wretched of deaths."[19] "The ancients considered death by crucifixion to be not just any execution, but the most obscene, the most disgraceful, the most horrific execution known to man."[20]

Yet this is the form of death chosen by God for Himself. Perhaps this suggests something about God's perspective on sin, and its enormity when opposed to infinite holiness and infinite love.

Now Jesus is nailed to the cross.

The "nails" were actually tapered iron spikes about seven inches long and a half inch across. In the wrists,

> the driven nail would crush or sever the rather large sensorimotor median nerve. The stimulated nerve would produce excruciating bolts of fiery pain in both arms....Most commonly, the feet were fixed to the front of the stipes [the vertical section of the cross] by means of an iron spike driven through the first or second intermetatarsal space....It is likely that the [major] nerves would have been injured by the nails.[21]

The pain would be unimaginable.

On the Cross

Here begins the worst of Jesus' torment:

> When the victim was thrown to the ground on his back, in preparation for transfixion of his hands, his scourging wounds most likely would become torn open again and contaminated with dirt. Furthermore, with each respiration, the painful scourging wounds would be scraped against the rough wood of the stipes. As a result, blood loss from the back probably would continue throughout the crucifixion ordeal.[22]
>
> Once crucified to the cross, the criminal was then thrown to the ground on his back, with arms out-stretched along the patibulum. A fall with the heavy

patibulum on His back may have led to a contusion of the heart, predisposing His heart to rupture on the cross. When the cross was erected upright, there was tremendous strain put on the wrists, arms and shoulders, resulting in a dislocation of the shoulder and elbow joints.[23]

Shallowness of breathing causes small areas of the lungs to collapse. The psalmist prophesied all this a thousand years beforehand: "I am poured out like water, and all my bones are out of joint. My heart has turned to wax; it has melted away within me. My strength is dried up like a potsherd, and my tongue sticks to the roof of my mouth; you lay me in the dust of death" (Psalm 22:14-15). To add to the horror, "not uncommonly, insects would light upon or burrow into the open wounds or the eyes, ears, and nose of the dying and helpless victim, and birds of prey would tear at these sites."[24]

The Passion of the Christ accurately, if generically, depicts all this. Given the power of the portrayal, it's not surprising that a few moviegoers actually had heart attacks and died in the theater. Others apparently committed suicide shortly after viewing the film.

Nearly everyone knows what it's like not to be able to breathe: frightening and horrible simultaneously. Extreme difficulty in breathing is one of the worst aspects of crucifixion, bringing a continuous series of agonies (presumably, about every 30 seconds). It is a vicious cycle: one must breathe to survive, but one cannot breathe without inflicting dreadful self-torture. But because of the pressure exerted on the lungs by the weight of the body, the victim must push upward in order to breathe. But this forcibly rubs the lacerated back against the rough wooden cross; it places agonizing pressure on the feet and wrists and brings various searing pains throughout the body. The following is more medically specific:

Adequate exhalation required lifting the body by pushing up on the feet and by flexing the elbows and adducting the shoulders. However, this maneuver would place the entire weight of the body on the tarsals [the small bones at the top of the foot] and would produce searing pain. Furthermore, flexion of the elbows would cause rotation of the wrists about the iron nails and cause fiery pain along the damaged median nerves.[25]

At this point, as the arms fatigue, great waves of cramps sweep over the muscles, knotting them in deep, relentless, throbbing pain. With these cramps comes the inability to push Himself upward....[The chest] muscles are paralyzed and the [rib] muscles are unable to act. Air can be drawn into the lungs, but cannot be exhaled. Jesus fights to raise Himself in order to get even one short breath. Finally, carbon dioxide builds up in the lungs and in the bloodstream and the cramps partially subside. Spasmodically, He is able to push Himself upward to exhale and bring in the lifegiving oxygen. It was undoubtedly during these periods that He uttered the seven short sentences recorded.[26]

Everything Jesus does on the cross increases His pain. He cannot even speak without torture: "Christ spoke seven times from the cross. Since speech occurs during exhalation, these short, terse utterances must have been particularly difficult and painful."[27]

Not surprisingly, crucifixion is where we get the word *excruciating*: "Death by crucifixion was, in every sense of the word, excruciating (Latin, *excruciatus,* or 'out of the cross')."[28] The entire ordeal—beatings, flogging, crucifixion—left Jesus so marred that He was actually *unrecognizable* as a human being—perhaps explaining the failure of some people to recognize Him at first after His resurrection.[29] Isaiah foretold of many who were appalled at Him—"his appearance was so disfigured beyond that of any man and his form marred beyond human likeness" (Isaiah 52:14).

What Goes Beyond Our Comprehension

And yet we know nothing of what *actually* happened on the cross. Not during the hidden hours when darkness covered the whole land and Jesus could not be seen—not even during the time He was physically visible. We have at best a feeble glimpse of the *real* torture. The "mere" bodily sufferings of Jesus have no comparison, in any way, to the almost infinite psychic and spiritual sufferings He endured in love for those for whom He was dying—willingly enduring the full wrath of God at all human sin through all the ages. These sufferings must remain silent with the Lord, unspoken (Deuteronomy 29:29).

> The LORD has laid on him the iniquity of us all....It was the LORD's will to crush him and cause him to suffer (Isaiah 53:6,10).
>
> God so loved the world that he gave his one and only Son, that whoever believes in him shall not perish but have eternal life (John 3:16).

But now the simple words of the Gospels can have more meaning for us: "When they came to the place called the Skull, there they crucified him."

But even as He was crucified, Jesus did not think of Himself. He prayed *for* those who were callously murdering Him: "Father, forgive them, for they do not know what they are doing" (Luke 23:34). Author and journalist John Zmirak comments pointedly about this:

> The most wondrous miracle Jesus performed through-
> out His life—which converts one of the Romans who
> crucified Him, on the spot—was His forgiveness,
> freely bestowed, in the midst of hideous suffering, on
> His tormentors. Such courage and generosity are liter-
> ally superhuman—yet they answer to man's deepest
> need, to the darkest squalid corner in each of our
> hearts which we "know" is irredeemable, which we
> yearn to bring out into air and light, and heal. In this
> film we see with unbearable clarity how Jesus
> descended into the personal Hell each of us carries
> around, and purged it clean.[30]

While Jesus is literally dying for others' sins, He is cruelly
taunted and insulted by nearly everyone present: Those who
pass by Him "hurled insults"; all the religious leaders—the
chief priest, elders, and teachers of law—"mocked him"; even
the robbers who were crucified with Him "also heaped insults
on him" (Matthew 27:39-44). In sheer moral idiocy the religious leaders shout, "He saved others...but he can't save himself....Let him come down now from the cross and we will
believe in him" (verse 42). Like a lamb led to slaughter, Jesus
never says a word. At some point, one of the criminals shows
more sense than the religious authorities. He reconsiders his
actions and repents: "Jesus, remember me when you come into
your kingdom." Again not thinking of Himself despite His torment, Jesus answers, "I tell you the truth, today you will be
with me in paradise" (Luke 23:42-43).

From noon until three P.M. "darkness came over all the
land" (Matthew 27:45). About the time it ends, Jesus cries out,
"My God, my God, why have you forsaken me?" In all the
Gospel accounts, only here does He not refer to God as His
Father. Then saying, "It is finished," He cries out in a loud
voice, "Father, into your hands I commit my spirit." He willingly

gives up His spirit and expires: The relentless torment is finally over (John 19:30; Luke 23:46).

Both heaven and earth react to Jesus' death.

> At that moment the curtain of the temple was torn in two from top to bottom. The earth shook and the rocks split. The tombs broke open and the bodies of many holy people who had died were raised to life. They came out of the tombs, and after Jesus' resurrection they went into the holy city and appeared to many people.
>
> When the centurion and those with him who were guarding Jesus saw the earthquake and all that had happened, they were terrified, and exclaimed, "Surely he was the Son of God!" (Matthew 27:51-54).

An earthquake that splits large boulders would get anyone's attention. But perhaps it alone would not bring about the response of the Romans. However, seeing tombs break open and living people emerge indeed terrifies them and causes them to exclaim that this *is* God's Son.

The miraculous top-to-bottom tearing of the great innermost curtain of the temple, made of the royal colors of blue, purple, and scarlet (Exodus 26:31-35), may be the greatest symbol of all. Access to the Most Holy Place, the presence of God Himself, is now freely available (see Hebrews 9). But the raising of many saints from the dead who later enter Jerusalem and appear to many people is, like the resurrection, without

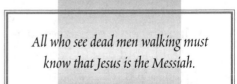

All who see dead men walking must know that Jesus is the Messiah.

parallel in history. All who see dead men walking *must* know that Jesus is the Messiah.

Many of Jesus' disciples are watching all this from a distance (Matthew 27:45-55); they see Jesus' death and its incredible aftermath. The emotional impact of this upon them must have been stunning, but we are not given details. Joseph of Arimathea now goes boldly before Pilate to request Jesus' lifeless body. The governor is surprised to hear that Jesus has died so soon, as prisoners often lingered on the cross for days. He summons the centurion to confirm Jesus' death and then gives the body to Joseph.

Certainly weeping, Joseph takes Jesus' battered and unrecognizable body from the cross and lays Him in his own new garden tomb. Jesus is buried with about 75 pounds of spices, in strips of linen "in accordance with Jewish burial customs" (John 19:39-40). A very large stone is rolled across the face of the tomb.

It's done.

The Jewish leaders, though apparently not all present at the crucifixion, couldn't be more satisfied. The very one they had so long sought to kill is now dead. But they wish to protect their treachery to the end. They go to Pilate and request that a Roman seal and guard be placed at the tomb. "We remember that while he was still alive that deceiver said, 'After three days I will rise again.' So give the order for the tomb to be made secure until the third day. Otherwise, his disciples may come and steal the body and tell people that he has been raised from the dead. This last deception will be worse than the first" (Matthew 27:62-64). Pilate gives the orders to make the tomb as secure as possible; the Roman seal is placed on the stone at the entrance, and the Roman guard is posted, making tampering impossible.

Despite the miracles at the moment of Jesus' death, not a soul suspects anything and not a single disciple understands what is shortly to occur....

After the Passion: The Rest of the Story Emerges

After the passion everything changes. As powerful and unparalleled as the film *The Passion of the Christ* is, it is principally about the *passion* of the Messiah. It covers the very last hours of the Messiah's life—"brief" hours that forever altered what was to come. (Those 12 hours, incidentally, took 12 years for Mel Gibson to conceive, produce, and film.)

But the *resurrection* of the Messiah—the celestial exclamation point to the passion—is only briefly glimpsed in the movie. Yet it covers all eternity. If *The Passion* has a major weakness, it might be this. Perhaps people will be confused about the blood-soaked brutality, not comprehending that *because* Jesus rose from the dead, the passion becomes the most magnificent message to them ever—supplying literal proof that their sins have been forgiven and that eternal life is a free gift now available through faith in Christ.

The passion *without* the resurrection would be senseless brutality on the scale Gibson portrays, and justifying some of the criticism of the film. But if *The Passion of the Christ* underscores the love God has for us, the resurrection underscores the absolute proof of this love. In that sense, even with all the history and evidence involved, this is a story about love.

This book picks up where *The Passion* leaves off for the reason that the resurrection of Jesus Christ is the most powerful and most central fact of history—the fact without which no other fact makes sense. The apostle Paul preached "Christ crucified," but he went on to emphasize that if the resurrection didn't happen, then nothing matters (see 1 Corinthians 1:23;

15:12-20). And because it did happen, everything in life and history is forever altered.

Considering the Competition

Christianity has become the most compelling and persuasive philosophy in history because it is based entirely upon the bedrock fact of the resurrection, which proves biblical faith true. For two millennia, this has been the foundation from which contrary religions and philosophies have been so powerfully subdued.

In all the world, with its thousands of competing religions, *only* the crucifixion and resurrection of Christ truly demonstrate that there is a God who loves us—and then prove the infinity and eternality of that love. The result is that the jaws of other religions and philosophies are wired shut. They now have little to say because the death and resurrection of Christ say everything. And if the crucifixion is terrible news for Jesus but wonderful news for everyone else, the resurrection is wonderful news for Jesus and incredible news for everyone else. It proves beyond doubt who Jesus is, and that the one grave dilemma of humanity—dreadful sin separating us from the presence of a holy God—can be fully forgiven, forever.

No one else has this message. No one has anything coming even close to this message. Other religions have whatever they have—but if they truly have proof of anything new or important, it has never been presented. The Christian faith, though, presents the dying and atoning incarnate God, brought back to life forever as a guarantee of our eternal salvation—the Good News carrying an eternal exclamation point. And all of it offered as a free gift—no merit or deeds of any sort required. That's *especially* why it's good news! Other faiths have no news at all, universally teaching salvation by merit—but Christianity stands alone. It is unique in the claims it makes and in its teachings.* Its founder is incomparable. In the manner of its salvation and the evidence it offers for its claims, the Christian faith is matchless.

When one religion stands above the rest, the sincere person need not examine all possible worldviews in an effort to find the truth. Nor need he or she conclude that all truth is relative merely because the contenders are numerous. Biblical Christianity leaves us few options: the evidence on which it rests can neither be invalidated nor ignored. Therefore, the one thing we must never do is attempt salvation on our own terms, and by so doing reject God's terms. Those who think they can stand on their own merit or power before an infinitely holy God are welcome to try. But that's the bad news about religion in general. When an impossible task is demanded, one's only guarantee is failure. The really good news, however, is that the resurrection of Jesus Christ is the keystone of God's saving plan for all humanity.

Implications of the Resurrection

We believe the historical evidence will lead an impartial investigator to conclude that Christianity alone is fully true—because of the resurrection of Jesus Christ from the dead. What are the implications for the human race, past, present, and future?

- *The resurrection gives proof that Jesus is who He claimed to be.* Jesus is the prophesied Messiah, the one and only Son of God (God incarnate), and the Lord and Judge of all the living and the dead.[31]

- *The resurrection gives proof that faith in Jesus secures eternal salvation as a permanent possession.* This includes forgiveness of all sins, past, present, and future; personal justification (that is, the righteousness of Christ is

---

* For more on this point, see appendix A.

eternally credited to the believer's account); and assurance of future resurrection to eternal life.[32]

- *The resurrection gives proof to all people of future judgment.* This judgment is based on our response to Christ in this life, which is the determining factor as to whether our sins are forgiven or remain to be judged.[33] As Acts 17:30-31 makes clear, "God commands all people everywhere to repent. For he has set a day when he will judge the world with justice by the man he has appointed. He has given proof of this to all men by raising him from the dead."

- *The resurrection gives proof that Christ alone is the way to God.* Jesus taught, "I am the way and the truth and the life. No one comes to the Father except through me" (John 14:6). No other way is acceptable to God, because only Christ atoned for human sin. Only Christ rose from the dead in proof of His atonement for sin. Only Christ is God's Son (John 3:16,18); therefore, only Christ is God's chosen way to salvation. For all that God has done for people, He asks no more than that they trust in His Son for their salvation and not in themselves—or in others who claim to offer salvation apart from this kind of proof.[34]

No better news exists anywhere. No simpler or securer path to heaven can ever be found. If Jesus Christ did indeed physically rise from the dead, then His claims on our life deserve our allegiance above those of any other.

"Forced to Make a Decision"

"Between us and heaven or hell there is only life, which is the frailest thing in the world," as Blaise Pascal noted. Only the resurrection offers proof that we can have safety—which from this vantage point, is why its importance surpasses even that of the atonement. Without the resurrection, no one can know the meaning of the atonement. Indeed it has no meaning.

"Moviegoers will be forced to make a decision about Christ after they leave the theater." Earlier, we quoted those words of *The Passion of the Christ*'s director, Mel Gibson. In the following chapters we offer you the evidence for something even more profound than Christ's passion, if that were possible. And even more than the passion, Christ's resurrection confronts us with a decision. After the darkest night of Death, the brightest sunrise of Life emerges, offering nothing less than the possibility of the perfect ending to every person's life—and death.

If only it were true, many skeptics have said.

This book shows why the resurrection really is true, and why life finds its most profound meaning because of it.

PART I

EVIDENCE FOR THE RESURRECTION

A man rising from the grave is an object of sense and can give the same evidence of his being alive as any other man in the world can give. So that a resurrection considered only as a fact to be proved by evidence is a plain case; it requires no greater ability in the witnesses than that they be able to distinguish between a man dead and a man alive: a point in which I believe every man living thinks himself a judge.

THOMAS SHERLOCK

The Tryal of the Witnesses
of the Resurrection of Jesus (1729)

THE RESURRECTION OF CHRIST is central to establishing or disproving the Christian religion. For instance, the French rationalist Charles Guignebert, at one time Professor of the History of Christianity at the Sorbonne, utterly repudiated belief in Christ's resurrection along with all miracles. He nonetheless acknowledged:

> There would have been no Christianity if the belief in the Resurrection had not been founded and systematized....The whole of the soteriology and the essential teaching of Christianity rests on the belief of the Resurrection, and on the first page of any account of Christian dogma might be written as a motto Paul's declaration: "And if Christ be not risen, then is our preaching vain, and your faith is also vain." From the strictly historical point of view, the importance of belief in the Resurrection is scarcely less.[1]

Likewise, the first great modern rationalistic interpreter of the New Testament, David Friedrich Strauss, conceded that the resurrection is "'the Touchstone...of Christianity itself' and is 'decisive for the whole view of Christianity.'"[2]

The writers of the New Testament trace back the belief in the resurrection to the claims of Jesus Himself. Jesus *publicly* announced He would rise from the dead and even the specific time He would do so—on the third day. In the field of comparative religions, this is unique. No one else in their normal mind has ever made such claims. But Jesus did on numerous occasions:

- During His Galilean ministry, Jesus replied to some Jewish leaders, "An evil and adulterous generation craves for a sign; and yet no sign shall be given to it but the sign of Jonah the prophet; for just as Jonah was three days and three nights in the belly of the sea monster, so shall the Son of Man be three days and three nights in the heart of the earth" (Matthew 12:39-40).

- After Peter's confession of Jesus as the Messiah, we are told that Jesus "began to teach them that the Son of Man must suffer many things and be rejected by the elders and the chief priests and the scribes, and be killed, and after three days rise again" (Mark 8:31; see also Matthew 16:21; Luke 9:22).

- Following the transfiguration, Jesus predicted, "The Son of Man is going to be delivered into the hands of men; and they will kill him, and he will be raised on the third day" (Matthew 17:22-23; see also Mark 9:31).

- After the cleansing of the temple, Jesus told the Jews in Jerusalem, "Destroy this temple, and in three days I will raise it up" (John 2:19). John then adds that "he was speaking of the temple of his body" (verse 21).

- Before His triumphal entry into Jerusalem, Jesus again predicted the events: "All things which are written through the prophets about the Son of Man will be accomplished. For he will be delivered to the Gentiles, and will be mocked and mistreated and spit upon, and after they have scourged him, they will kill him; and the third day he will rise again" (Luke 18:31-33; see also Matthew 20:18-19; Mark 10:33-34).

- Jesus even predicted the specific *day* of His death by crucifixion: "You know that after two days the Passover is coming and the Son of Man is to be delivered up for crucifixion" (Matthew 26:2).

- Immediately after the Last Supper, when the disciples had gone to the Mount of Olives, Jesus told them,

"You will all fall away because of me this night, for it is written, 'I will strike down the shepherd, and the sheep of the flock shall be scattered.' But after I have been raised, I will go before you to Galilee" (Matthew 26:31-32; see also Mark 14:28).

The cumulative weight of these predictions is immense. On the above occasions and on others, Jesus predicted He was to die and be raised from the dead. *Such claims have no precedent or parallel in human history.*

Further, the specific content of the predictions is noteworthy:

1. Jesus would rise from the dead by His *own* power (John 2:19; 10:18).

2. He would endure much suffering before His death (Mark 8:31); He would be mocked, mistreated, spit upon, and whipped (Luke 18:32-33).

3. The elders and chief priests would reject Him (Mark 8:31).

4. The events would transpire in Jerusalem (Matthew 20:18).

5. The chief priests and scribes would condemn Him to death and deliver Him up to the Roman authorities to be killed (Matthew 20:18-19).

6. His death and resurrection would fulfill *all* the Old Testament prophecies concerning Him (Luke 18:31-33).

7. He would die specifically by crucifixion (Matthew 26:2).

8. He knew *to the day* when this would occur (Matthew 26:2).

9. All the disciples would fall away, despite their emphatic claims of allegiance to Him (Matthew 26:31-35; see also Mark 14:27-31).

10. He knew *exactly* when He would return from the dead—"on the third day" (Luke 18:33).

How could a mere man know such things? How could He be so specific? How could Jesus be certain He would not die by natural or accidental causes, or be executed in some other way? How did He know He would die by crucifixion on the Passover in Jerusalem? How did He know all His followers would desert Him? How could He claim that He would fulfill all that the prophets had to say about Him (scores or hundreds of prophecies), or that He had the power to conquer death? How could He predict the exact *day* He would rise from the dead?

The only adequate explanation is that Jesus was who He claimed He was—the divine Savior of the world. Had He failed in any *one* of these predictions, He would have been shown to be wrong, and His claim to be God would have been proven false (see John 5:16-18; 10:27-33).

In the next four chapters we will concentrate on the New Testament evidence for the resurrection, and also include evidence from secular history, logic, and law.[3] We will show that the biblical evidence is trustworthy and vindicates Jesus' claims about Himself: *The events surrounding His death came to pass exactly as He had predicted.*

2

JESUS' DEATH AND BURIAL—
AND THE EMPTY TOMB

❦

MANY HISTORIANS AND NEW TESTAMENT scholars accept as fact certain key events surrounding Jesus' death. They commonly agree that

- Jesus actually died
- His body was placed in a grave whose location was well known, even to His enemies
- Roman soldiers guarded the tomb at the request of the Jewish leaders
- the tomb was later empty

These historical points form a unit. Together they provide compelling evidence that Jesus rose from the dead.

The Death of Jesus

The evidence indisputably affirms that Jesus really died. The greatest proof of this is the open nature of His crucifixion:

Jesus was put to death in a great public execution known to such historians as Tacitus and Josephus. The execution was in the capital of the Jewish commonwealth under the direction of the Roman governor and his soldiers, in cooperation with the highest Jewish authorities, and during one of the great religious seasons. Jesus certainly died....According to the Gospels the grave-owner was known, the type of burial is known, its location was known. When Pilate set a watch over the grave he indicated its locality to friend and foe alike.[1]

The following details of the crucifixion enhance this picture and help us to understand better why so few doubt that Jesus actually died:

1. Jesus was crucified publicly according to standard Roman practice (John 19:18), a practice both severe and chillingly efficient. (We have already examined this process in detail in chapter 1.) Condemned criminals were deliberately placed on public display as a warning to everyone that they must obey Roman law and authority. Thus the events were commonplace and public: A squad of four Roman executioners put Jesus to death before a large crowd of onlookers.

2. Roman soldiers remained by the cross, as indicated by their casting lots for Jesus' garments. Matthew mentions that "they *kept watch* over him there" (Matthew 27:36 NIV) and that "the centurion and those with him…were *guarding* Jesus" (verse 54 NIV). Since death by crucifixion was so horrible, guards were necessary lest family and friends remove a condemned man from the cross and spare him the agony and torment. Furthermore, part of a soldier's sworn duty was to make certain that the crucified prisoner died.

3. Dozens of Jesus' friends and enemies watched Him die on the cross. Everyone present heard His death cry (Mark 15:39-41; Luke 23:44-49).

4. Jewish law prohibited the body of a condemned man to remain on the cross during the Sabbath (Saturday). Since the crucifixion occurred on Friday morning, the Jews requested Pilate to have the prisoners' legs broken, bringing immediate death through suffocation (John 19:31). Their bodies could, therefore, be removed from the cross before the Sabbath began at 6 P.M. Friday. Pilate granted the request; the soldiers broke the legs of the two men on either side of Jesus (verse 32). But these same soldiers—practiced in determining whether a crucified man was dead or alive— "when they saw that He was already dead, they did not break His legs" (verse 33; see also verse 36; Numbers 9:12; Psalm 34:20).

5. Since it was unusual for a crucified man to die this quickly, a soldier pierced Jesus' side with a spear to be doubly sure He was dead. We are told that "immediately blood and water came out" (John 19:34). The mixture of blood and water medically confirms that the sword had pierced Jesus' heart and that He had already died.[2]

6. Pilate had the centurion *reconfirm* that Jesus was dead. The only way the Roman governor could legally release the body to Joseph of Arimathea was to have Jesus' death verified: "Joseph of Arimathea...went boldly to Pilate and asked for Jesus' body. Pilate was surprised to hear that he was already dead. Summoning the centurion, he asked him if Jesus had already died. When he learned from the centurion that it was so, he gave the body to Joseph" (Mark 15:43-45 NIV).

7. The commanding centurion had personally heard Jesus' death cry and had also seen the spear thrust into His side (Mark 15:39; John 19:34).

8. The apostle John observed Jesus' death firsthand and recorded the entire series of events, including the death cry and the spear thrust, in his Gospel. Immediately following his account of Jesus' death, John states, "He who has seen has testified, and his testimony is true; and he knows that he is telling the truth, so that you also may believe" (John 19:35).

In other words, John makes it perfectly clear to his readers that, on the basis of eyewitness testimony, Jesus *had* died on the cross. This means that the only valid explanation for Jesus' subsequent appearances is the resurrection itself.

Was Survival Even Possible?

At this point we should consider again all that Jesus went through.

- He underwent six trials, which included beatings and a scourging that alone sometimes killed people.
- He carried the heavy crossbeam to the crucifixion site.
- He underwent the horrible tortures of the crucifixion itself.
- He had a sword thrust through His side, piercing His heart.

As we just noted, His death was confirmed by Roman soldiers and then again by the centurion himself to one no less than Pilate.

Survival of crucifixion was unknown, just as surviving the firing squad, the electric chair, a lethal injection, or the gas chamber is unheard of today. Because the law had decreed the prisoner's death, even if a first attempt failed, procedures would be repeated until the decree was carried out. But death from crucifixion was as certain as any modern method of execution. There was no escape.

> Josephus (*Vita,* 75) tells of a time when he saw a number of captives being crucified; and, noticing three of his friends among them, he asked Titus, the Roman commander, for a reprieve. This was granted, and the men were taken down at once. It seems that they had only just been crucified, but despite being given every care by the most expert physicians available, two of the three died....There can be no doubt that Jesus was dead.[3]

Further, the centurion who oversaw Jesus' execution was in all likelihood a man of superior intellect. Centurions in the Roman army were experienced soldiers, specially selected for their ability and alertness. Because of their experience on the battlefield and at executions, they were experts in the art of killing and knew how to determine if a man were dead.[4] The centurion's comment that "truly this man was the Son of God!" (Mark 15:39), significant enough in the fact it came from a Roman unbeliever, also shows by the

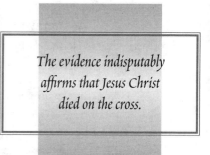

The evidence indisputably affirms that Jesus Christ died on the cross.

past tense of the verb ("was") that in the soldier's judgment, Jesus was already dead. Indeed, had he given a false report of this fact to Pilate, it would have cost him his life.

Those who removed Jesus' body and buried it would certainly have noticed any signs of life. Had He been alive, they would not have *buried* Him—they would have done everything in their power to *save* Him. But all the accounts agree that Jesus was buried according to Jewish custom, with 75 pounds of spices and linens used for the embalming.

The above evidence, especially the public nature of the execution, helps explain why more than 1,800 years passed before someone proposed the nonsense that Jesus really did not die on the cross.[5] No one could possibly have put forth such a theory on the day of the crucifixion itself.

All four Gospel writers agree that Jesus died on the cross (Matthew 27:50; Mark 15:37; Luke 23:46; John 19:30). The fact is repeated many times in the book of Acts and the epistles.

In conclusion, the evidence indisputably affirms that Jesus Christ died on the cross. But the fact He was later seen alive by dozens of eyewitnesses in many different locations over a period of 40 days cannot be explained apart from the resurrection.

The Burial of Christ

The facts surrounding the burial of Christ give further proof that not only was Christ dead, but that it would have been impossible for anyone to take the body. The apostle John reports that Joseph of Arimathea came and removed Jesus' body from the cross. In addition,

> Nicodemus, who had first come to him by night, also came, bringing a mixture of myrrh and aloes, about a hundred pounds weight [literally 100 *litres*, 12 ounces each]. So they took the body of Jesus and bound it in linen wrappings with the spices, as is the burial custom of the Jews. Now in the place where He was crucified there was a garden, and in the garden a new tomb in which no one had yet been laid. Therefore because of the Jewish day of preparation, since the tomb was nearby, they laid Jesus there (John 19:39-42).

Wilbur M. Smith points out that we know more about Jesus' burial than we do of any other person in ancient history:

We know infinitely more about His burial than we do about the burial of any Old Testament character, of any king of Babylon, pharaoh of Egypt, any philosopher of Greece, or triumphant Caesar.

We know who took His body from the cross; we know something of the wrapping of the body in spices, and burial clothes; we know the very tomb in which His body was placed, the name of the man who owned it, Joseph, of a town known as Arimathaea. We know even where the tomb was located, in a garden nigh to the place where He was crucified, outside the city walls. We know minute details concerning events immediately subsequent to our Lord's entombment, that a stone was rolled against the tomb, that this stone was sealed, and that, by the wish of the Jews, Roman guards were set before the tomb to prevent the body being stolen. We have four records of this burial of our Lord, all of them in amazing agreement.[6]

Jesus' friends and enemies had carefully observed the location of the place where Jesus was buried (Matthew 27:61,66). The spectacle of the Roman guard stationed in front of the tomb would also have drawn public attention to it. As with His death and burial, the location of Jesus' grave was public knowledge, freely available to anyone. If Christ had not risen, it could easily have been proven He was still dead and in the grave.

Precautions for Guarding the Tomb

Once Jesus was entombed, the Jewish authorities took extraordinary measures to ensure that the body could not be moved or stolen. Jesus' enemies were well aware of His prediction that He would rise from the dead on the third day, and as far as they were concerned, this could only come about if the disciples were to steal the body. Therefore, they made certain that no one could even approach the tomb. Matthew reports,

> Now on the next day, the day after the preparation, the chief priests and the Pharisees gathered together with Pilate, and said, "Sir, we remember that when He was still alive that deceiver said, 'After three days I am to rise again.' Therefore, give orders for the grave to be made secure until the third day, otherwise His disciples may come and steal Him away and say to the people, 'He has risen from the dead,' and the last deception will be worse than the first." Pilate said to them, "You have a guard; go, make it as secure as you know how." And they went and made the grave secure, and along with the guard they set a seal on the stone (Matthew 27:62-66).

The Jewish authorities were highly motivated. They had gone to great lengths in their conspiracy against Jesus. They were convinced He was a blasphemer whose followers and teachings must be permanently suppressed.

> The authorities had a deep underlying fear of Jesus. This is one of the most brilliant conclusions of Frank Morison's famous book *Who Moved the Stone?* It was not only that they had feared an uprising by the people, which Jesus could easily have provoked at that time of excitement, but they feared Jesus' own powers.[7]

To safeguard their interests, the Jewish leaders arranged for a Roman guard to protect the tomb. They made it as secure as possible, even placing an official seal on the stone covering the entrance.

The Jews called the gravestone a *gloal*. The *gloal* protected the deceased against the ravages of both man and beast. Such a stone usually weighed from one to two tons and required several men to move it.[8] In this case, a stone toward the upper limit was probably selected. An indication that this was the case can be seen from a parenthetical phrase in Codex Bezae (currently in the Cambridge Library holdings), an early copy of the Scriptures. Written next to Mark 16:4, the phrases stated that the stone against the tomb was one "which twenty men could not roll away."[9] Mark records that the stone was "extremely large" (16:4). The women who had observed Jesus' body being put into the tomb and the stone being rolled across its mouth (see Matthew 27:60-61) knew that it was too large for them to move. This is evident from their statement: "Who will roll away the stone for us from the entrance of the tomb?" (Mark 16:3).

The tomb was secured, furthermore, by a Roman seal. "The sealing was done in the presence of the Roman guards who were left in charge to protect this stamp of Roman authority and power."[10] The seal was the equivalent of the United States government seal; its very presence would have prevented tampering by all but the most foolhardy. Anyone attempting to move the stone would have broken the seal and thus incurred the wrath of Rome.

In addition, the presence of the guard virtually guaranteed that Jesus' body could not have been stolen. To be caught asleep at his post meant certain death for a Roman sentinel in the highly disciplined Roman guard:

> The punishment for quitting [one's] post was death according to the laws....The most famous discourse on the strictness of camp discipline is that of Polybius... which indicates that the fear of punishments produced faultless attention to duty, especially in the night watches.[11]

Additional ancient testimony indicates that the death penalty was required for desertion, disobedience in wartime, losing or disposing of one's arms, or taking flight when the example would influence others.[12]

When we consider the penalties each Roman guard knew he would incur, the extensive weaponry each one carried,[13] the guards' extensive military training and expertise, and their devotion to the Roman seal, all these indicate that no human source removed the body. It took nothing less than an angel from heaven to frighten the soldiers into a state of powerlessness (Matthew 28:2-4).

In all probability, this marked the first time in Roman history that a guard had been assigned to watch the grave of a publicly crucified criminal. Everything humanly possible had been done to ensure that Jesus' body could not be stolen. Upon reaching their post, the *first* thing the guard most likely did was inspect the tomb and make certain everything was in order—that the body was still there.

But later, these same soldiers reported to the chief priests that the tomb they were guarding was now empty (Matthew 28:11-13)!

The Empty Tomb

Many people saw Jesus die and knew where He was buried. Some of them saw His body placed in the tomb, the rock rolled across the entrance, the tomb sealed, and the Roman soldiers placed on duty to guard it.

But no one at all, at any time, at any place, has ever doubted that the tomb was found empty.

> No man has written, pro or con, on the subject of Christ's resurrection, without finding himself compelled to face this problem of Joseph's empty tomb.

That the tomb was empty on Sunday morning is recognized by everyone, no matter how radical a critic he
may be. However antisupernatural in all his personal
convictions, he never dares to say that the body was still
resting in the tomb, however he might attempt to
explain the fact that the tomb must have been empty.[14]

In addition, the Jewish authorities apparently never questioned the guards' report that the tomb was empty (Matthew
28:11-15). They knew the guards would not have come back
with such a story unless what they reported was true. But
because of the seriousness of the report, the authorities most
likely went to the tomb to examine it personally. Once they
saw the tomb was indeed empty, the gravity of the situation
became clear to them.

To many of them, Jesus was a false messiah. They had made
a great effort to be rid of Him.[15] We should also remember that
Jesus had thousands of followers and had performed stupendous miracles unlike any other prophet in Jewish history (for
example, John 9:32). He had also stood trial before Jewish and
Roman authorities (Matthew 26:57-66; 27:1-2,12-14).

This new messianic movement had directly threatened
Jewish interests and power. The Pharisees and chief priests themselves had admitted that Christ's following was so great that "the
world has gone after Him" (John 12:19). They had therefore
plotted to kill Him because they feared that "if we let Him go on
like this, all men will believe in Him, and the Romans will come
and take away both our place and our nation" (John 11:48).

In light of this, once the apostles proclaimed that the grave was
empty and that Christ had been resurrected, the Jewish leaders
doubtless made a search for the body. But it was never found.
As Jesus prophesied, they would search for His body, but not be
able to find it (John 7:34; 8:21).

A Safe Assumption

The reality of the empty tomb makes the case for the resurrection more than credible. For instance, "A.M. Ramsey
wrote, 'I believe in the Resurrection, partly because a series of
facts are unaccountable without it.' The empty tomb was 'too
notorious to be denied,'"[16] and had any doubts existed concerning it, they would certainly have been widely circulated.
But there were none.

> All the references to the empty tomb come in the
> Gospels, which were written for Christians who
> wanted to know the facts. In the public preaching to
> those who were not yet convinced, as recorded in the
> Acts of the Apostles, there was an insistent emphasis on
> the resurrection, but not a single reference to the
> tomb. For this I can see only one explanation. There
> was no point in speaking of the empty tomb, for
> everyone—friend and foe alike—knew that it was
> empty. The only points worth arguing about were
> why it was empty, and what its emptiness proved.[17]

The apostles preached throughout Jerusalem both day and
night that Christ had risen from the dead (Acts 5:28), an event
so radical that it eventually changed the world. It would have
been easy to discredit such preaching merely by producing
Jesus' body.

> If Jesus had not arisen, there would have been evi-
> dence that he had not. His enemies would have
> sought and found this evidence, but the apostles went
> up and down the very city where he had been cruci-
> fied and proclaimed right to the faces of his slayers
> that he had been raised, and no one could produce
> evidence to the contrary. The very best they could do
> was to say the guards went to sleep and the disciples
> stole the body while the guards slept.[18]

The silence of Jesus' enemies, therefore, is as eloquent a proof of the resurrection as is the apostles' proclamation.

The Burial Wrappings

The position of Jesus' graveclothes supplies further evidence that the empty tomb means that Jesus rose. Their position is intriguing. When John first looked into the empty tomb, "he saw and believed" (John 20:8). What was it about the graveclothes that made a skeptic conclude that Jesus had risen? (John and the other disciples did not understand Jesus' claim that He would rise from the dead—see, for example Mark 9:10,32; Luke 18:34.) Was it not the fact that the wrappings remained only as a shell—as if the body had disappeared from within them, leaving only an empty hull?

> Peter went into the tomb; he saw the linen cloths lying, and the napkin, which had been on his head, not lying with the linen cloths but rolled up in a place by itself...and he (i.e., the other disciple) "saw and believed" (John 20:6-8). Why should this have made such an impression upon the two disciples? Because the wrappings seemed to them like a chrysalis case when the pupa has emerged. The graveclothes had encircled Jesus, and were interlaced with a great weight of embalming spices. The head covering was a small distance away, retaining its original shape surrounding the head of Jesus. *But his body was simply gone!* No wonder they were convinced and awed. No graverobber would have been able to enact so remarkable a thing. Nor would it have entered his head. He would simply have taken the body, graveclothes and all. Had Jesus merely been resuscitated, he would presumably either have used the clothes or laid them aside. But as it was, all the signs pointed to Jesus' having risen to a

new order of life, a new sphere of existence. He left the
graveclothes behind as the butterfly emerging to a new
dimension of life leaves the cocoon behind it. That
sight convinced Peter and John.[19]

Enshrining the Dead

Another piece of evidence supports that the tomb was
empty. It is natural to venerate great religious leaders. Throughout history, religious pilgrim-
ages have been made to special
shrines honoring dead prophets or teachers, especially
their birth or burial places.
Muslims have their yearly pil-
grimage to Mecca. Every year
Hindus and Buddhists visit
the graves of their noted gurus.
Indeed, even the graves of
Jewish holy men were carefully
noted and honored. But in the
history of Christianity, such
has never occurred for Jesus.

*Throughout history, religious
pilgrimages have been made
to special shrines honoring dead
prophets or teachers.... In the
history of Christianity, such has
never occurred for Jesus.*

We cannot find in the contemporary records any trace
of a tomb or shrine becoming the center of veneration
or worship on the ground that it contained the relics
of Jesus. This is inconceivable if it was ever seriously
stated at the time that Jesus was really buried else-
where than in the vacant tomb. Rumor would have
asserted a hundred supposititious places where the
remains really lay, and pilgrimages innumerable
would have been made to them.[20]

When Christians go to see Christ's tomb in Jerusalem, they know they go to see an *empty* tomb. William Lane Craig summarizes some of the evidence under the following points:

- the historical reliability of the burial accounts
- the independent testimony of the apostle Paul
- the impossibility of proclaiming the resurrection in Jerusalem unless the tomb were empty
- the earliest Jewish propaganda against Christians, which presumes the empty tomb (the stolen-body theory)

The conclusion is, "It is extremely difficult to object to the empty tomb on historical grounds; those who deny it do so on the basis of theological or philosophical assumptions [like the assumption that miracles are impossible]....No natural hypothesis can furnish a plausible explanation....This alone would justify our accepting the resurrection as the simplest, most probable explanation of the empty tomb."[21]

Further,

> It is impossible that [the disciples] would have sacrificed their possessions and their blood in the service of Christ if their announcement of His resurrection had been based upon deceit. How could the ineradicable joy, certainty and power have come into their lives after His crucifixion if their whole faith were a gigantic lie? Everything points to the fact that there is only one explanation for the empty sepulchre: Jesus' claim to be the Son of God was true, and no bonds of death and darkness could keep Him confined to the grave. He did arise, and He lives.[22]

In summary, we have strong grounds for believing that the tomb of Jesus Christ was empty. And every theory proposed to explain the empty tomb is much more difficult to believe than the one that biblical evidence, viewed logically, indicates—that Jesus Christ rose physically from the dead.*

* For more discussion on the alternate attempts to explain the resurrection, see appendixes B and C.

3

Jesus' Resurrection
Appearances

⬥

In considering Jesus' resurrection appearances, we must keep in mind their relationship to the empty tomb. The resurrection appearances *alone* would have been worthless hallucinations unless the tomb was indeed empty. If Jesus' body had ever been found, it would have revealed the apostles' encounters with the "resurrected" Jesus as merely visionary. In other words, only the empty tomb allows for the resurrection appearances and only the resurrection appearances adequately explain the empty tomb. They are two sides to the same coin.

Eyewitness Nature of the Testimony

The testimony of those people who witnessed Jesus' postresurrection appearances is critical. Several undeniable facts about them arise:

1. Many of the disciples and all of the apostles testified that they had personally witnessed Jesus' resurrection.

2. The disciples firmly adhered to Jewish law, which required true testimony on penalty of divine judgment.

3. For the rest of their lives the apostles and many disciples faced much persecution and, in some cases, eventual martyrdom for testifying to Jesus' resurrection from the dead.

These three facts converge to provide strong evidence for the resurrection.

The Witnesses Spoke Out

Many of the disciples and all of the apostles testified that they had witnessed Jesus' resurrection. *The Oxford American Dictionary* defines "witness" as one "who gives evidence in court" and "who is present at an event in order to testify to the fact that it took place." A witness does not give "hearsay," but "something that serves as evidence"—direct evidence. It is not opinion, conjecture, supposition, or anything less than evidence personally and carefully attested to by the one who saw it.

The apostles repeatedly point out that the events of Christ's death and resurrection were well known. While on trial, Paul emphasizes the empirical nature of the case for Christ's resurrection when he states that he speaks words "of sober truth" concerning matters that have "not been done in a corner" (Acts 26:25-26; see also 2:22). Abundant eyewitness testimony was available to confirm Jesus' life, death, and resurrection, and the apostles' frequent appeal to such evidence affirms this.

John's account. In his Gospel, the apostle John states that "he who *has seen* has *testified,* and his testimony *is true*" (19:35). His account ends with the words, "This is the disciple who is *testifying* to these things and wrote these things, and *we know* that his testimony *is true*" (21:24).

Writing many years after the resurrection, John continues to emphasize in his letters the eyewitness nature of the case.

He knew he had seen the risen Jesus and that nothing in the intervening period had changed his mind:

> That which was from the beginning, which we have heard, which *we have seen* with our eyes, which *we have looked at* [the two emphasized verbs connote *to scrutinize; examine carefully; to behold intelligently;* they express a "definite investigation by the observer" (Westcott)[1]] and our hands *have touched*—this we proclaim concerning the Word of life. The life appeared; we have seen it and *testify* to it, and we proclaim to you the eternal life, which was with the Father and has *appeared* to us. We proclaim to you what we have *seen* and *heard* (1 John 1:1-3 NIV).

Peter's words. The apostle Peter remarks, "We did not follow cleverly devised tales when we made known to you the power and coming of our Lord Jesus Christ, but we were *eyewitnesses* of His majesty" (2 Peter 1:16).

Luke's reports. Luke clarifies that his own accounts also come from *eyewitness testimony* (the Greek word for "eyewitness" in Luke 1:2 literally means "one who beholds for himself"):

> Many have undertaken to draw up an account of the things that have been fulfilled among us, just as they were handed down to us by those who *from the first were eyewitnesses* and servants of the word. Therefore, since I myself have *carefully investigated everything from the beginning,* it seemed good also to me to write an orderly account for you, most excellent Theophilus, so that you may *know the certainty* of the things you have been taught (Luke 1:1-4 NIV).

Five important points emerge for our discussion from this passage:

1. When Luke says "the things that have been fulfilled among us" (verse 1), he is referring to Jesus' life and the things He said and did.

2. Eyewitnesses to Jesus' life went on to testify of what they had seen and heard. Luke acknowledges his dependence upon these eyewitnesses.

3. Luke mentions that his predecessors' testimony did not remain oral. It was written down—"many have undertaken to draw up an account" (verse 1). He writes yet another account on the basis of oral and written testimony drawn from these firsthand witnesses.

4. Luke states his qualifications for writing his book, namely, that he had "carefully investigated everything from the beginning" (verse 3). He gives the impression here that he personally double-checked the information he had received against other reliable sources.

5. Luke purposed to give Theophilus—probably a high-ranking Roman official (indicated by the phrase "most excellent," verse 3)—certainty as to what he had been told about Christianity (verse 4). The resurrected Jesus displays a similar concern: "After his suffering, he showed himself to these men and gave *many convincing proofs* that he was alive. He appeared to them over a period of *forty days* and spoke about the kingdom of God" (Acts 1:3 NIV). Furthermore, according to the Gospel tradition, the resurrected Jesus told the disciples, "You are *witnesses* of these things" (Luke 24:48; see also Acts 1:8; John 15:27).

Early apostolic preaching also repeatedly emphasized the *eyewitness* nature of the resurrection to both Jew and Gentile, believer and skeptic:

- Acts 2:32: "This Jesus God raised up again, to which *we are all witnesses.*"

- Acts 3:15: "You...put to death the Prince of life, the one whom God raised from the dead, a fact to which we are *witnesses.*"

- Acts 4:33: "With great power the apostles were giving *testimony* to the resurrection of the Lord Jesus."

- Acts 5:30,32: "The God of our fathers raised up Jesus, whom you had put to death...and we are *witnesses* of these things."

- Acts 10:37-43: *"You yourselves know* the thing which took place throughout all Judea, starting from Galilee, after the baptism which John proclaimed. *You know of* Jesus of Nazareth, how God anointed Him with the Holy Spirit and with power, and how He went about doing good and healing all who were oppressed by the devil, for God was with Him. *We are witnesses* of all the things He did both in the land of the Jews and in Jerusalem. They also put Him to death by hanging Him on a cross. God raised Him up on the third day and granted that He become visible, not to all the people, but to witnesses who were chosen beforehand by God, that is, to us *who ate and drank* with Him after He arose from the dead. And He ordered us to preach to the people, and *solemnly to testify* that this *is the One* who has been appointed by God as Judge of the living and the dead. Of Him *all the prophets bear witness* that through His name everyone who believes in Him receives forgiveness of sins."

- Acts 13:29-33: "When they had carried out all that was written concerning Him, they took Him down from the cross and laid Him in a tomb. But God raised Him from the dead; and for *many days* He appeared to those who came up with Him from Galilee to Jerusalem, the very ones who are now His *witnesses* to the people. And we preach to you the good news of the promise made to the fathers, that God has fulfilled this promise to our children in that He raised up Jesus."

- Acts 17:30-31: "God is now declaring to men that all people everywhere should repent, because He has fixed a day in which He will judge the world in righteousness through a Man whom He has appointed, *having furnished proof to all men by raising Him from the dead.*"

In modern criminal trials, most juries are convinced by two corroborating eyewitness testimonies to an event, and sometimes by only one. When prosecutors have three such eyewitnesses, their chances for a conviction rise to 99 percent. But for the resurrection we have far more than three eyewitnesses. We have such an abundance of corroborating eyewitness testimony that the chances are excellent a *modern* jury would conclude in favor of the resurrection even though it happened almost 2,000 years ago.*

Truth Was Paramount

The disciples firmly adhered to Jewish law, which required true testimony on penalty of divine judgment. The apostles' frequent appeal to eyewitness testimony is all the more striking, if it were false testimony, in light of their own Jewish heritage. No religion stressed the importance of truth or a truthful testimony more than the Jewish religion.

---

* See further pages 100–105.

In the Old Testament Scriptures, God repeatedly warned Israel against falsehood; a false witness was evil and worthy of punishment. Each of the apostles knew that if they gave false testimony concerning Jesus' resurrection, they would be guilty of testifying falsely about God Himself (as Stephen was wrongly accused of—see Acts 6:8-14), a deed for which God would punish them and call them to account in the next life.

The Jewish law, given by God Himself, would encourage sober reporting on the part of the apostles. For example:

- Exodus 20:16: "You shall not bear false witness."

- Exodus 23:1: "You shall not bear a false report; do not join your hand with a wicked man to be a malicious witness."

- Deuteronomy 17:6: "On the evidence of two witnesses or three witnesses, he who is to die shall be put to death; he shall not be put to death on the evidence of one witness."

- Deuteronomy 19:15-19: "A single witness shall not rise up against a man on account of any iniquity or any sin which he has committed; on the evidence of two or three witnesses a matter shall be confirmed. If a malicious witness rises up against a man to accuse him of wrongdoing, then both the men who have the dispute shall stand before the LORD....The judges shall investigate thoroughly, and if the witness is a false witness and he has accused his brother falsely, then you shall do to him just as he had intended to do to his brother."

- Proverbs 19:5,9: "A false witness will not go unpunished, and he who tells lies will not escape....He who tells lies will perish" (see also Proverbs 21:28).

The background of the Jewish law helps us better understand why the apostle Paul emphasized the importance of being *certain* of Christ's resurrection and, correspondingly, the consequences of false testimony: "If Christ has not been raised, then our preaching is vain, your faith also is vain. Moreover we are even found to be *false witnesses of God*, because we testified against God that He raised Christ" (1 Corinthians 15:14-15).

Consequences to the Witnesses

For the rest of their lives, the disciples faced much persecution and, in some cases, eventual martyrdom for testifying about Jesus' resurrection from the dead. Would they have gone through persecution, prison, and eventual martyrdom for what was a lie? And if they were deceived, some of them would most assuredly have come to their senses and exposed the belief in Jesus' bodily resurrection as a piece of fiction. But nothing of the sort happened. Here is a sampling of some of the kinds of things they endured:

- Acts 4:1-3: "As they were speaking to the people, the priests and the captain of the temple guard and the Sadducees came up to them, *being greatly disturbed* because they were teaching the people and *proclaiming in Jesus the resurrection from the dead*. And they laid hands on them and *put them in jail*."

- Acts 5:18: "They laid hands on the apostles and put them in a *public jail*."

- Acts 5:40: "After calling the apostles in, they *flogged them* and ordered them to speak no more in the name of Jesus."

- Acts 8:1,3: "Saul was in hearty agreement with putting him [Stephen] *to death*. And on that day a *great persecution* began against the church in Jerusalem....Saul began *ravaging* the church, entering house after house, and *dragging off* men and women, he would put them *in prison.*"

- Acts 12:1-3: "Herod the king laid hands on some who belonged to the church in order to mistreat them. And he had James the brother of John *put to death* with a sword....He proceeded to *arrest Peter* also."

- Acts 23:12-13: "The Jews formed a conspiracy and bound themselves under an oath, saying that they would neither eat nor drink until they had *killed Paul.* There were more than forty who formed this plot."

But despite persecution, imprisonment, and even execution, "every day, in the temple and from house to house, they kept right on teaching and preaching Jesus as the Christ" (Acts 5:42). They not only continued to proclaim that they had directly witnessed the risen Christ but claimed that the Old Testament prophets, God Himself, and the Holy Spirit also testified about Him:

- Acts 10:43: "Of Him all the prophets bear witness" (see also Romans 3:21).

- 1 John 5:9-10: "The testimony of God is this, that He has testified concerning His Son. The one who believes in the Son of God has the testimony in himself; the one who does not believe God has *made Him a liar,* because he has not believed in the testimony that God has given concerning His Son."

- Acts 5:32: "We are witnesses of these things; and so is the Holy Spirit, whom God has given to those who obey Him."

People simply do not die for what they know is false. Almost all of the original apostles became martyrs, apparently meeting death by some of the cruelest of methods: James, the brother of Jesus, was stoned to death; Peter, Andrew, Philip, Simon, Bartholomew and James the son of Alphaeus were crucified; Matthew and James the son of Zebedee died by the sword; Thaddaeus was killed by arrows; and Thomas met death by a spear thrust. Evidently only John died of natural causes.[2]

In light of all this, it is difficult to imagine that the disciples were perpetuating a hoax. This is totally inconsistent with what is known about the moral quality of their lives. These men were committed Jews who believed in the divine moral prescriptions of the Old Testament Scriptures and who condemned lying and stressed honesty. They could be harassed, thrown in prison, flogged, beaten, and killed, but they could not be made to deny their conviction that Jesus had risen from the dead.

The Extent and Nature of the Resurrection Appearances

The New Testament cites 12 appearances of the resurrected Jesus: 11 between the period of Easter morning and His ascension 40 days later, and one later appearance to Paul on the Damascus road. These appearances

> are as well authenticated as anything in antiquity.... There can be no rational doubt that they occurred, and that the main reason why Christians became sure of the resurrection in the earliest days was just this. They could say with assurance, "We have seen the Lord." They *knew* it was He.[3]

> Indeed, so strong is the evidence for these appearances that Wolfhart Pannenberg, perhaps the world's greatest living systematic theologian, has rocked modern, skeptical German theology by building his entire theology

precisely on the historical evidence for the resurrection of Jesus as supplied in Paul's list of appearances.[4]

The 12 appearances are as follows:

1. to the women as they returned from the tomb after having seen the angel who had informed them that Christ had risen (Matthew 28:1-10)

2. to Mary Magdalene, during her second visit to the tomb that morning (John 20:10-18; Mark 16:9-11)

3. to Peter sometime before the evening of the resurrection day, but under circumstances the details of which are not given (Luke 24:34; 1 Corinthians 15:5)

4. to Cleopas and another disciple on the road to Emmaus on Easter afternoon (Luke 24:13-35; Mark 16:12-13)

5. to 10 of the apostles with others whose names are not given (Thomas is absent), gathered together at their evening meal on Easter Sunday (Luke 24:36-40; John 20:19-23; 1 Corinthians 15:5; Mark 16:14-18)

6. a week later to all 11 apostles, including Thomas (John 20:26-28)

7. to some of the disciples fishing on the Sea of Galilee, the time undesignated (John 21:1-23)

8. to the apostles on a specific mountain in Galilee (Matthew 28:16-20)

9. to James, with specific information as to time and place not stated (1 Corinthians 15:7)

10. to the apostles on the Mount of Olives at Jerusalem just prior to the ascension (Luke 24:50-52; Acts 1:3-8; Mark 16:19)

11. to 500 more believers all at once (1 Corinthians 15:6)

12. to Paul on the Damascus road (1 Corinthians 15:8; Acts 9:1-9)

Four important characteristics emerge from this list: 1) the great variety of the appearances, 2) their indisputable physical and empirical nature, 3) the varied temperaments of the individuals to whom Jesus appeared, and 4) the lack of time for legends about appearances to develop.

The Great Variety of the Appearances

Among Christ's appearances, the circumstances, the time, the place, and the individuals to whom He appeared vary considerably. He appeared to women, men, groups, individuals, and to more than 500 people at once; He appeared by an open lake, on a mountain, on a road, in the upper room behind locked doors, and in country, town, and hillside. All these appearances comprise abundant testimony which must be taken seriously.[5]

Jesus did not appear to merely one person or once to a single group; He revealed Himself to individuals on numerous occasions and to different groups at many different times in many different locations.

> *If anybody had been fabricating the appearances, they would not have made the first witnesses of the resurrection those to whom credibility was not readily granted.*

Moreover, Jesus' first appearance was to women. This is unusual, as it was not in accord with Jewish tradition. "One of the oldest commentaries on the Law of Moses rejects testimony from a woman (*Siphre* on Deuteronomy, 190)."[6] If anybody had been fabricating the appearances, they would not have made the first witnesses of the resurrection those to whom credibility was not readily granted (see also John 4).

The Appearances Were Physical and Empirical

The chart on the next page serves to emphasize the physical—as opposed to visionary or metaphysical—nature of the resurrection appearances.

Every appearance mentioned in the Gospels is of a physical, bodily kind. This is especially impressive considering the independent nature of the accounts, which

> were originally more or less separate, independent stories, which the different gospel writers collected and arranged in order. All their separate sources of information agree that Jesus appeared physically and bodily to the disciples and other witnesses.
>
> There is no trace of nonphysical appearances in the sources, a remarkable fact if all the appearances were really visionary, as some critics would have us believe. That strongly suggests that the appearances were not in fact visions, but actual, bodily appearances. The very fact that all the separate gospel stories agree on that point, and that no trace of visionary "appearances" is to be found, weighs strongly in favor of the gospels' historical credibility in this matter.[7]

Moreover, Jesus' appearances do not fit any of the characteristics of visions or mass hallucinations as is commonly reported by individuals who work in this field of inquiry and who have compared the characteristics of hallucinations and visions with the New Testament record.[8]

The Appearances Were to Individuals of Widely Varying Temperaments

Thomas was an absolute skeptic, and most of the other disciples were doubtful upon first hearing of the resurrection appearances. Some found it difficult to believe even when they

The Appearances of Christ[9]

Persons	Saw	Heard	Touched	Other Evidence
Mary (Magdalene— John 20:10-18)	X			Empty tomb
Mary and women (Matthew 28:1-10)	X	X		Empty tomb
Peter (1 Corinthians 15:5; see also John 20:3-9; Luke 24:34)	X	X*		Empty tomb, grave clothes
John (John 20:2-10)				Empty tomb, grave clothes
Two disciples (Luke 24:13-35)	X	X		Ate with Him
Ten apostles (Luke 24:36-49; John 20:19-23)	X	X	X**	Death wounds
Eleven apostles (John 20:24-31)	X	X	X**	Death wounds
Seven apostles (John 21)	X	X		Ate with Him
All apostles (Matthew 28:16-20; Mark 16:14-18)	X	X		Ate with Him
500 brethren (1 Corinthians 15:6)	X	X*		
James (1 Corinthians 15:7)	X	X*		
All apostles (Acts 1:4-8)	X	X		
Paul (after ascension— Acts 9:1-9; 1 Corinthians 15:8)	X	X		

* Implied
** Offered to be touched

actually *saw* Jesus. The women departing the empty tomb did so with fear, apprehension, and great joy. Mary Magdalene was confused and wept at the tomb. The disciples on the road to Emmaus were melancholic and despondent. Several disciples had given up and returned to their old occupation as fishermen. These are normal and expected emotions under the circumstances; their diversity argues for their soberness and genuineness, not for their fabrication.

The Lack of Time for Legendary Appearances to Develop

A chief problem faced by critics who attempt to discount the physical appearances is that they must account for how the stories of these appearances came about. If the critic considers them mere visions or pure fiction, he must assume that much, if not all, of their content stems from later Christian embellishment. This idea, however, is not credible.

> The time was too short for legends of Jesus' physical appearances to accumulate,...the presence of the living eyewitnesses to the appearances would have served as a control against false accounts of what happened,...the authoritative control of the apostles would have served to preserve the accurate accounts. If the appearances were originally only visions, then those three factors would have prevented them from being perverted into physical appearances. It is inexplicable how a series of mere visions could be so thoroughly materialized and corrupted into the unanimous physicalism of the gospel appearance stories in so short a time, in the presence of the very witnesses to those appearances themselves, and under the eyes of the apostles responsible for preventing such corruption.[10]

Reinforcing this point, other appearances of Christ may have gone unreported. For instance, after Jesus appeared to Thomas, John reports that Jesus performed many additional attesting miracles in *the presence of the disciples* that were not recorded (John 20:30-31).

When the apostles preached that Christ had been resurrected, they did so on the basis of having personally seen Him. They were convinced that even Christ's enemies had no reasonable grounds for doubt (Acts 4:13-14). As Wilbur Smith notes, "At a moment when it was yet possible to test every incident, to examine every witness, and to expose every trace of fraud, the Apostles openly and unhesitatingly proclaimed the fact."[11]

Imagine today dozens of people, all credible witnesses and initial skeptics, claiming to have seen the late former President Ronald Reagan risen from the dead in a wide variety of circumstances and locations. Imagine, moreover, that more than 500 Republicans claimed to have seen him at the same time and place. Every one of these claimed appearances could be checked out.

In a parallel sense, Paul boldly told the skeptics of his day, "Look, several hundred witnesses of the risen Christ are still alive. Go ask them yourself what they saw. See if they are deluded or lying" (1 Corinthians 15:6; see also Acts 26:22-29; 1 Corinthians 15:3-8,12-19).

> Confronting a learned and hostile hierarchy who had opposed Jesus bitterly during His lifetime, the apostles did not dare to make indefensible assertions. To claim falsely that Jesus had risen from the dead would expose

them to ridicule and would invite disaster to their cause. They were too astute to offer to the public baseless legends or wild dreams as the initial proof of their new faith.

The Gospels and Epistles...agree unanimously... that His physical presence was attested by competent witnesses, who were willing to stake their lives on the fact that He had risen.[12]

In summary, no theory adequately explains Jesus' resurrection appearances except the one espoused by the apostles themselves—that these instances were literal, physical appearings of Jesus risen from the dead.

4

The Powerful Evidence
of Skepticism

⚜

Certain aspects of first-century (and later) Christianity remain inexplicable apart from Jesus' bodily resurrection and subsequent appearances to His followers. Among them are

- the apostles' transformation from skepticism to belief

- the birth and growth of the first-century church

- the change of the sacred day of worship among Jewish converts from Saturday to Sunday and the origin of the Christian sacraments of baptism and the Lord's Supper

- the testimony of former skeptics

The Apostles' Transformation
from Skepticism to Belief

The resurrection appearances were so convincing that they transformed the lives of the disciples—and they in turn transformed the world. Great effects have great causes. That Jesus appeared to the disciples as a group at least three times sufficiently convinced even the most skeptical among them (John 21:14).

The disciples were indeed skeptics. Thomas refused to believe unless he could actually see Jesus and touch His wounds: "The other disciples were saying to him, 'We have seen the Lord!' But he said to them, 'Unless I see in His hands the imprint of the nails, and put my finger into the place of the nails, and put my hand into His side, I will not believe'" (John 20:25). Though many consider Thomas the most skeptical of the disciples, the others, according to all four Gospels, doubted almost as much.

When Jesus appeared to Thomas, he at least immediately believed, saying to Jesus, "My Lord and my God!" (John 20:28). But some of the other disciples apparently struggled to believe even after Jesus had personally appeared to them! The stupendous nature of the resurrection miracle made it difficult to absorb quickly. According to Matthew's Gospel, *"The eleven disciples proceeded to Galilee, to the mountain which Jesus had designated. When they saw Him, they worshiped Him; but some were doubtful"* (28:16-17). Considering the circumstances, though, such skepticism is understandable.

Another skeptic was in all probability Jesus' own brother James (Mark 3:20-21; 6:3; John 7:3-5). This also is understandable. If Jesus were your brother, what would it take to convince you that He, whom you had been with for almost 30 years and had then personally seen publicly executed, had now risen from the dead? Would you believe right away, even if you saw Him? Or would it—at least initially—be almost beyond your ability to accept?

Josh McDowell comments,

> When Jesus was alive, James didn't believe in his brother Jesus as the Son of God (John 7:5). He as well as his brothers and sisters may even have mocked

> him....For James it must have been humiliating for
> Jesus to go around and bring ridicule to the family
> name by his wild claims ("I am the way, and the
> truth, and the life; no one comes to the Father, but
> through Me"—John 14:6)....What would *you* think
> if your brother said such things?
>
> But something happened to James. After Jesus was
> crucified and buried, James was preaching in Jerusa-
> lem....Eventually James became one of the leaders of
> the Jerusalem church and wrote a book, the epistle of
> James. He began it by writing, "James, a servant of
> God and of the Lord Jesus Christ." His brother. Even-
> tually James died a martyr's death by stoning at the
> hands of Ananias the high priest....Was James
> deceived? No, the only plausible explanation is 1 Co-
> rinthians 15:7—"there he [Jesus] appeared to James."[1]

Mary Magdalene also did not believe the resurrection at
first. She thought that somehow, someone had removed the
body: "[The angels] said to her, 'Woman, why are you
weeping?' She said to them, 'Because they have taken away my
Lord, and I do not know where they have laid Him'" (John
20:13). According to Mark's Gospel, after Jesus appeared to
her, she went and reported to the disciples that He had risen.
But "they were mourning and weeping....When they heard
that He was alive and had been seen by her, they *refused* to
believe it" (16:11).

Then, after Jesus appeared to the two disciples on the road
to Emmaus, they went and reported this meeting to the other
disciples, but "they did not believe them either" (verse 13). In
fact, the disciples were so reluctant to believe the news that
Jesus was alive that when He appeared to them He had to
rebuke them for their unbelief: "Afterward He appeared to the
eleven themselves as they were reclining at the table; and He

reproached them for their unbelief and hardness of heart, because they *had not believed those who had seen Him* after He had risen" (verse 14).

Luke records in his Gospel the discussion between the two disciples on the road to Emmaus and a stranger, whom they initially were prohibited from recognizing as Jesus:

> We were hoping that it was He who was going to redeem Israel. Indeed, besides all this, it is the third day since these things happened. But also some women among us amazed us. When they were at the tomb early in the morning, and did not find His body, they came, saying that they had also seen a vision of angels who said that He was alive. Some of those who were with us went to the tomb and found it just exactly as the women also had said; but Him they did not see (24:21-24).

Jesus rebuked them for their unbelief: " 'O foolish men and slow of heart to believe in all that the prophets have spoken! Was it not necessary for the Christ to suffer these things and to enter into His glory?' Then beginning with Moses and with all the prophets, He explained to them the things concerning Himself in all the Scriptures" (verses 25-27).[2]

He shortly thereafter rebuked the Eleven as well for their lack of faith in His resurrection:

> They were startled and frightened and thought that they were seeing a spirit. And He said to them, "Why are you troubled, and why do doubts arise in your hearts? See My hands and My feet, that it is I Myself; touch Me and see, for a spirit does not have flesh and bones as you see that I have." And when He had said this, He showed them His hands and His feet. While they still could not believe it because of their joy and

amazement, He said to them, "Have you anything here to eat?" They gave Him a piece of broiled fish; and He took it and ate it before them (verses 37-43).

Convinced Against Their Will

We can hardly overestimate how devastating the crucifixion was to the disciples. It destroyed their hope that Jesus was the expected Messiah (Luke 24:21). They had, moreover, sacrificed much for Jesus, including their jobs, reputations, and families (Matthew 19:27 and parallel passages). Everything of value was pinned squarely on Him: all their hopes, their entire lives, everything—but now He was dead, branded a criminal.

Jesus went to great lengths to convince His skeptical followers He had indeed risen from the dead. Only after He had appeared to them again and again, talking and eating with them, encouraging them to touch Him to see that He had a physical body, showing them the wounds in His hands and side, did they

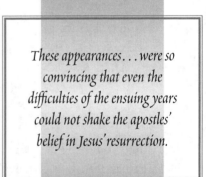

These appearances... were so convincing that even the difficulties of the ensuing years could not shake the apostles' belief in Jesus' resurrection.

become convinced. In the end, the disciples believed and were filled with great joy (Luke 24:41,52-53; John 20:20). Had we been in their place, we would probably have reacted in much the same way.

Only Jesus' physical resurrection appearances satisfactorily explain the marked transformation of His followers from skepticism to belief. These were people who were not ready to believe: *They were convinced against their will.* If they *had* expected a resurrection, they would have been waiting and ready to receive it openly. But they were not expecting this (Matthew 28:17; Luke 24:25-27,38-41; John 20:24-27). They needed a lot of convincing when it happened—40 days' worth (Acts 1:3).

These appearances, however, were so convincing that even the difficulties of the ensuing years could not shake the apostles' belief in Jesus' resurrection. They testified to it even in death. Lawyer Irwin H. Linton notes,

> So strong an assurance of truth and sincerity accompanies the declarations of a man who truly believes he is then and there dying that the law admits such declarations as testimony even though to do so violates two major rules of the law of evidence: that against "hearsay" and the prohibition against testimony which has not been subjected to the test of cross-examination.[3]

Birth and Growth of the First-Century Church

How could the church ever have come into existence from the disheartened, frightened, disillusioned band of Jesus' followers?

The Gospel tradition makes it clear none of the disciples understood the need for the resurrection. This can be seen in Peter's rebuke of Jesus when He predicted His death and resurrection (Matthew 16:21-22 and parallel passages). Furthermore, they did not understand what Jesus meant by it. When Jesus predicted His resurrection after the transfiguration, Mark says of the disciples who were with Jesus, "they did not understand this statement, and they were afraid to ask Him" (9:32). In Mark 9:9-10, after Jesus spoke of His rising from the dead, we are told that "they seized upon that statement, discussing with one another what rising from the dead meant." After all, people just don't rise from the dead. Their ignorance about the resurrection, in fact, seemed divinely intended. For example, on another occasion when Jesus spoke of His resurrection, the disciples "understood none of these things, *and the meaning of this statement was hidden from them,* and they did not comprehend the things that were said" (Luke 18:34).

How then do we account for their belief in something which was completely unexpected? And in turn, for the birth and growth of the church? William L. Craig discusses how a mysterious "something" must be proposed to explain the origin of Christianity:

> It is quite clear that without the belief in the resurrection the Christian faith could not have come into being. The disciples would have remained crushed and defeated men. Even had they continued to remember Jesus as their beloved teacher, His crucifixion would have forever silenced any hopes of His being the Messiah. The cross would have remained the sad and shameful end to His career. *The origin of Christianity therefore hinges on the belief of the early disciples that God had raised Jesus from the dead....*
>
> Now the question becomes: What caused that belief? As R.H. Fuller says, even the most skeptical critic must presuppose some mysterious *X* to get the movement going. But what was that *X*?...Clearly, it would not be the result of Christian influences, for at that time there was no Christianity....
>
> But neither can belief in the resurrection be explained as a result of Jewish influences....The Jewish conception of resurrection differed in two important, fundamental respects from Jesus' resurrection. In Jewish thought the resurrection *always* 1) occurred after the end of the world, not within history, and

> 2) concerned all the people, not just an isolated individual. In contradistinction to this, Jesus' resurrection was both within history and of one person....
>
> The disciples, therefore, confronted with Jesus' crucifixion and death, would only have looked forward to the resurrection at the final day and would probably have carefully kept their master's tomb as a shrine, where His bones could reside until the resurrection.[4]

To explain sufficiently the origin of the belief in the resurrection apart from the fact that it happened is virtually impossible. Secular historians who study the events surrounding the origin of the church are left with no satisfactory answer if they reject the resurrection.

> According to C.F.D. Moule of Cambridge University, here is a belief nothing in terms of previous historical influences can account for. He points out that we have a situation in which a large number of people held firmly to this belief, which cannot be explained in terms of the Old Testament or the Pharisees, and that these people held onto this belief until the Jews finally threw them out of the synagogue.
>
> According to Professor Moule, the origin of this belief must have been the fact that Jesus really did rise from the dead.[5]

Can we really believe that, prior to the resurrection appearances, the disciples' frame of mind was at all inclined to invent the phenomenon of the church? Would the unbelieving and skeptical disciples have proclaimed, without physical confirmation, a resurrection they never expected in the first place? As commentator Norval Geldenhuys puts it,

It is historically and psychologically impossible that the followers of Jesus, who at His crucifixion were so completely despondent and perplexed, would within a few weeks thereafter enter the world (as they did) with such unheard-of joy, power and devotion, if it had not been for the fact that He had risen from the dead, had appeared to them, and had proved that His claims to be the Son of God were genuine.[6]

Other Peculiarities About the Church's Origin

Apart from the resurrection, the power and attraction of the infant church are also virtually impossible to explain:

That it was faith in the Resurrection of Christ, and the preaching of this stupendous truth, that gave the early church its power to win thousands and then millions of idolatrous citizens of the great Roman Empire for Christ, though vast multitudes of them in confessing their faith knew they were dooming themselves to torture and social ostracism, is recognized among all who have given any careful consideration to the intricate, difficult problems of the establishment of the Christian church in the Roman world.[7]

Even rationalists and secularists have seen this clearly: "Modernist Dr. H.D.A. Major, Principal of Ripon Hall, Oxford,...[stated] 'Had the crucifixion of Jesus ended His disciples' experience of Him, it is hard to see how the Christian church could have come into existence.'"[8]

Journalist Frank Morison points out, moreover, that it is strange that the church could have won so many converts if the resurrection had never occurred.

Now the peculiar thing about this phenomenon is that, not only did it spread to every single member of

the party of Jesus of whom we have any trace, but
they brought it to Jerusalem and carried it with
inconceivable audacity into the most keenly intellectual centre of Judea, against the ablest dialecticians of
the day, and in the face of every impediment a brilliant and highly organized camarilla [a group of secret
and scheming advisers] could devise.

And they won. Within twenty years the claim of
these Galilean peasants had disrupted the Jewish
church and impressed itself upon every town on the
Eastern littoral of the Mediterranean from Caesarea to
Troas. In less than fifty years it had begun to threaten
the peace of the Roman Empire.[9]

Some of the obstacles the early church had to overcome
were daunting. First, there was much opposition from certain
elements within Judaism. Jews who believed in Jesus were
thrown out of the synagogues, and many were shunned by
their families.

Second, misunderstanding of the gospel evoked persecution
from the pagan world. The early church endured barbarous
persecutions from Roman rulers such as Nero (54–68),
Domitian (81–96), and sometime later, Diocletian (303).
Christians were often accused of being atheists (because they
rejected the Roman pantheon of gods and idol worship), of
being antisocial because they rejected the immoral practices of
the day, and even of participating in cannibalism and ceremo-
nial murder (out of a misunderstanding of the Lord's Supper).

Third, internal divisions and the constant threat of false
teaching repeatedly pummeled the church (Acts 20:29-30).

These are only a few of the difficulties faced by the early
church. Even though it was a minority religion begun by 12
men, unsupported by any national culture, wholly dependent
upon the tolerance of the rulers for its survival, it endured and
prospered. It did so when all of the more prominent and

powerful religious cults of the day perished so utterly that their names are known today only to specialists and scholars—such as Mithraism, the cult of Isis, and so on.

> After making allowance for all natural causes such as the unique promise of eternal life, the futility of the pagan philosophies, the influence of political patronage, and a growing popular sympathy for a persecuted minority, the rise and growth of the church cannot be adequately explained apart from the resurrection.[10]

Without Jesus' bodily resurrection, certain questions pertaining to the birth of the church remain unanswerable. For example, every one of the 27 New Testament books is grounded on the conviction that Jesus rose from the dead. If the resurrection had never happened, how is this prevailing conviction to be explained?

Why, moreover, would the apostles face the hostility and persecution of the Jewish leaders by attempting to found a new movement based on the teachings of merely a condemned criminal? Why would they continue to follow and speak about a man who was obviously a fraud or worse in that He predicted He would come back to life but never did?

Finally, on what basis would the apostles proclaim this dead person *as God* when their entire religious training had taught them it was blasphemous to call a man God (John 5:18; 10:33)? Would not such preaching be unthinkable, completely contrary to their personal theological convictions?

Everyone admits that the disciples believed in Jesus' resurrection. Even skeptics admit this. But only Jesus' resurrection appearances adequately explain the disciples' motivation to devote the rest of their lives to preaching Christ and nurturing the church Christ had founded.

Change of the Day of Worship and the Origin of Baptism and the Lord's Supper

What would it take to change the July 4 date of the U.S. Independence Day celebration? It would probably require nothing short of a constitutional amendment. But it would have taken even more to change the Jewish sabbath from Saturday to Sunday, for that was a day instituted not by people in honor of their freedom, but by God in honor of His creation of the universe (Genesis 2:1-3; Exodus 20:8-11).

> It is impossible to exaggerate the importance of the sabbath in Judaism. It was inaugurated by express divine command to celebrate God's rest after creation.
>
> But these men managed to change it to Sunday, because Sunday was the day when Jesus rose from the dead, and they reckoned that the new creation which that signified was even more important than the creation remembered by the sabbath.[11]

The earliest Christian congregations were comprised primarily of thousands of converted Jews who were firmly attached to Saturday for the sabbath by their tradition. Furthermore, the leaders of the early church were Jews, and some were men like Paul who had strict Pharisaical training in Jewish law. "Only the fact that Jesus arose on a Sunday and exalted that day to be 'the day of the Lord' can explain why the old Jewish custom was given up and the first day of the week was accepted as the day of rest—in honour of the risen Christ."[12]

Baptism and the Lord's Supper

Christian baptism and the Lord's Supper could not have been instituted apart from a bodily resurrection, for both rest squarely on it. Baptism illustrates conversion, a personal re-creation of Christ's own death and resurrected life in the new believer (Romans 6:3-5). Likewise, communion commemorates Christ's death, a celebration based on the fact that Jesus conquered death, rose again, and is coming back (1 Corinthians 11:24-26).

Without the bodily resurrection, these sacraments would represent only a mockery of God. They would be complete lies: commemorating the resurrection of a person who was still dead and in the grave. The resurrection, on the other hand, perfectly explains their origin and the rationale for their observance.

Testimony of Former Skeptics

The Oxford American Dictionary defines *evidence* as "1) anything that establishes a fact or gives reason for believing something; 2) statements made or objects produced in a law court as proof or to support a case."

Almost all religions require belief despite the evidence; only Christianity demands belief because of the evidence (Acts 17:30-31). For example, little genuinely historical or objective evidence exists for the specific religious claims of Hinduism, Buddhism, and Islam. Even noted Buddhist scholars have conceded that little can be known about the actual teachings of the Buddha; ultimate reality is defined as the ineffable state of *nirvana*. Hinduism's Scriptures are replete with contradictions; the universe is merely the *lila/maya* of Brahman—God's illusory play. In Islam, hermeneutical, textual, and other problems in the Qur'an make it difficult to accept the Muslim

> *Genuine intellectual skeptics do not easily change their views, especially when dealing with claimed supernatural events.*

claim that it is a divine revelation or that Allah is the one true God.[13]

As scientist Henry Morris observes,

> As a matter of fact, the entire subject of evidences is almost exclusively the domain of *Christian* evidences. Other religions depend on subjective experience and blind faith, tradition and opinion. Christianity stands or falls upon the objective reality of gigantic supernatural events in history and the evidences therefor. This fact in itself is an evidence of its truth.[14]

The uniquely evidential nature of Christian truth-claims explains why many noted scholars (once former skeptics) now acknowledge that Christianity alone is fully true. For example, legal scholar John Warwick Montgomery emphasizes that "the evidence for the truth of Christianity overwhelmingly outweighs competing religious claims and secular world views."[15] The late Mortimer J. Adler, architect of the Great Books of the Western World, chairman of the Board of Editors of the *Encyclopedia Britannica,* and director of the Institute for Philosophical Research in Chicago, remarks, "I believe Christianity is the only logical, consistent faith in the world."[16]

One of the most powerful evidences for the truth of Christianity, in particular the resurrection, is the testimony of those who formerly were skeptics, some of whom had set out to disprove it. The kind of evidence required to bring a complete turnaround in a person's convictions must be great. Genuine intellectual skeptics do not easily change their views, especially when dealing with claimed supernatural events, and particularly when such events are nonrepeatable.

We are not saying that all or even most skeptics who have set out to disprove Christianity have been converted. Sufficient evidence will not convince a person against his or her will. As Jesus Himself observed, anyone who rejects the evidence at hand will not be persuaded, no matter how great such evidence is—even if someone rises from the dead (Luke 16:30-31). We have in mind skeptics who are fair with the evidence and are willing to trace it to its logical conclusions despite their biases.

Over the past 2,000 years, many skeptics have converted to Christianity, not on the basis of need, opinion, emotion, or subjective experience, but on the basis of hard evidence. These are people of considerable intellect, who have done their best to try and disprove the faith. *We believe the testimony of their conversions alone is sufficient to establish a credible case for Christianity.* In what follows, we present a sampling of such ancient and modern testimony.

Paul. Growing up in Tarsus, a center of learning, Paul (formerly Saul) probably became familiar with various Greek philosophies and religious cults. He was fluent in the Greek language and adept in debate and logic. At the age of 14 he was sent to Jerusalem to study under Gamaliel, the greatest Jewish rabbi of the period (Acts 22:3; probably the grandson of Hillel).

As a devout Pharisee, "advancing in Judaism beyond many of [his] countrymen, being more extremely zealous for [his] ancestral traditions" (Galatians 1:14), Paul intended not so much to disprove Christianity as to destroy it (verse 13). He was bitterly opposed to the Christian claims about Jesus and the resurrection; he persecuted many Christians, literally laying waste the church. For example:

- Acts 22:4-5: "I persecuted this Way to the death, binding and putting both men and women into prisons, as also the high priest and all the Council of the elders can testify."

- Acts 26:9-11: "I thought to myself that I had to do many things hostile to the name of Jesus of Nazareth. And this is just what I did in Jerusalem; not only did I lock up many of the saints in prisons, having received authority from the chief priests, but also when they were being put to death I cast my vote against them. And as I punished them often in all the synagogues, I tried to force them to blaspheme; and being furiously enraged at them, I kept pursuing them even to foreign cities."

- Galatians 1:13: "You have heard of my former manner of life in Judaism, how I used to persecute the church of God beyond measure and tried to destroy it."

Thus, when Stephen was being stoned to death for his testimony concerning Christ, Saul was there "in hearty agreement with putting him to death" and "began ravaging the church, entering house after house, and dragging off men and women, he would put them in prison" (Acts 8:1,3; see also 22:19-20). A short while later, Saul, "still breathing threats and murder against the disciples of the Lord, went to the high priest, and asked for letters from him to the synagogues at Damascus, so that if he found any belonging to the Way, both men and women, he might bring them bound to Jerusalem" (Acts 9:1-2; see also verse 13).

But "something" changed Saul so radically that the world has never quite gotten over it. Even the early Christians, after suffering such persecution at his hand, could not believe it. In Damascus after his conversion, he immediately

> began to proclaim Jesus in the synagogues, saying "He is the Son of God." All those hearing him continued to be amazed, and were saying, "Is this not he who in Jerusalem destroyed those who called on this name,

and who had come here for the purpose of bringing them bound before the chief priests?" But Saul kept increasing in strength and confounding the Jews who lived at Damascus by proving that this Jesus is the Christ. When many days had elapsed, the Jews plotted together to do away with him (Acts 9:20-23).

What was it that led such a skeptic and staunch enemy of the church to become one of its greatest defenders? It was the irrefutable evidence of a direct appearance of the risen Jesus Himself. Paul records this meeting and how it permanently changed his life: "Have I not seen Jesus our Lord?" (1 Corinthians 9:1; see also Acts 22:4-21; Galatians 1:11-24; 1 Corinthians 15:1-19).

We often do not fully realize the impact this once committed enemy of the church has had upon world history because of his encounter with the resurrected Jesus. His three missionary journeys and lifelong evangelism and church-planting work helped to change the Roman Empire and even the destiny of Western civilization. As historian Archibald MacBride puts it, "Beside his achievements...the achievements of Alexander and Napoleon pale into insignificance."[17]

Athenagoras. A second-century scholar, brilliant apologist, and the first to head the eminent School of Alexandria, Athenagoras originally intended to write against the faith, being "occupied with searching the Scriptures for arguments against Christianity," but instead was converted because of what he found.[18]

Augustine of Hippo. Augustine (354–430) was raised in a pagan environment. At the age of 12 he was sent by his parents to the advanced schools in Madaura, a center of pagan culture and learning. He later studied and taught rhetoric in

Carthage. He mastered the Latin classics, was deeply influenced by Plato, Neoplatonism, and Manicheanism, and was for a time a religious skeptic. But after carefully reading the Bible and hearing the sermons of Bishop Ambrose while in Milan, he converted to Christianity and became perhaps the greatest father of the Western church. His two most famous works are *The Confessions* and *The City of God;* but among his other writings were apologetic works such as *Against the Academics,* a critique of the academic religious skepticism of his day.[19]

George Lyttleton and Gilbert West. Moving to the modern era, in the mid-eighteenth century Lord George Lyttleton, a member of Parliament and Commissioner of the Treasury, and Gilbert West, Esquire, while at Oxford University, determined to attack the very basis of Christianity. Lyttleton set out to prove that Saul of Tarsus had never converted to Christianity, and West intended to demonstrate that Jesus had never risen from the dead.

Each had planned to take a year to establish their case. But as they proceeded, they concluded on the basis of the evidence that Christianity was true. Both became Christians. West went on to write *Observations on the History and Evidences of the Resurrection of Jesus Christ* (1747), and Lyttleton penned a lengthy work entitled *Observations on the Conversion of St. Paul* (1747).

The correspondence between the two men is revealing; it shows their continuing surprise at the quality of the biblical evidence,[20] from which West became fully convinced of the truth of the resurrection and Lyttleton became fully convinced of the genuine conversion of Paul.

Reflecting on this, Lyttleton wrote to West in 1761,

Sir, in a late conversation we had together upon the subject of the Christian religion, I told you that besides all the proofs of it which may be drawn from the prophecies of the Old Testament, from the necessary connection it has with the whole system of the Jewish religion, from the miracles of Christ, and from the evidence given of his reflection by all the other apostles, I thought the conversion and apostleship of Saint Paul alone, duly considered, was of itself a demonstration sufficient to prove Christianity a divine revelation.[21]

Frank Morison. In the 1930s, Frank Morison (the pseudonym of Albert Henry Ross), an English journalist, attempted to discover the "real" Jesus Christ. As a rationalist, he was convinced that the history of Jesus' life "rested upon very insecure foundations"—largely because of the influence of higher criticism upon him. Furthermore, he was dogmatically opposed to the miraculous elements in the Gospels. He was fascinated, nevertheless, with the person of Jesus, who was to him "an almost legendary figure of purity and noble manhood."

Morison decided to take the crucial "last phase" of Jesus' life and "strip it of its overgrowth of primitive beliefs and dogmatic suppositions, and to see this supremely great Person as He really was....It seemed to me that if I could come at the truth *why* this man died a cruel death at the hands of the Roman power, how He Himself regarded the matter, and especially how He behaved under the test, I should be very near to the true solution of the problem."[22]

But the book Morison ended up writing was not the one he set out to write. He came to believe that the "miraculous elements" in the Gospels were sober history. He proceeded to write one of the most able defenses of Jesus' resurrection of our time, entitled *Who Moved the Stone?* (1930). The evidence he encountered for Jesus' resurrection changed his initial skepticism and his entire life.

Josh McDowell. As a pre-law student McDowell was also skeptical of Christianity and believed that every Christian had two minds: one was lost, and the other was out looking for it. He was challenged to investigate intellectually the Christian truth-claims. Though thinking this a farce, he accepted the challenge and as a result, he "found historical facts and evidence about Jesus Christ that [he] never knew existed."[23] As a convert, he has written a number of well-known books defending Christianity; among them are *Evidence that Demands a Verdict* (1979), *More Evidence that Demands a Verdict* (1981), *More Than a Carpenter* (1983), and *Daniel in the Critics' Den* (1979).

John Warwick Montgomery. As a philosophy student at Cornell University, Montgomery was a convinced skeptic. He writes, "I went to university as a 'garden-variety' 20th-century pagan. And as a result of being *forced,* for intellectual integrity's sake, to check out this evidence, I finally came around."[24]

He tells of an obstinate undergraduate engineering student who continued to challenge him to *really* examine the evidence: "I thank God that he cared enough to do the reading to become a good apologist because if I hadn't had someone like that I don't know if I would have become a Christian."[25]

Montgomery went on to earn a PhD from the University of Chicago, and a second doctorate in theology, plus seven additional graduate degrees in theology, law, library science, and other fields. He has written more than 125 scholarly journal articles, plus 40 books, many of them defending the Christian faith against skeptical views. He is also one of the few lawyers admitted to practice in both England and America. People with the kind of background, temperament, and philosophical premises that Dr. Montgomery had simply do not believe in Christianity apart from sufficient evidence.

C.S. Lewis. The Oxford and Cambridge scholar C.S. Lewis, a former atheist, was converted to Christianity on the basis of the evidence, as he recounted in his book, *Surprised by Joy* (1955). He recalls, "I thought I had the Christians 'placed' and disposed of forever." But "a young man who wishes to remain a sound atheist cannot be too careful of his reading. There are traps everywhere—'Bibles laid open, millions of surprises,' as Herbert says, 'Fine nets and stratagems.' God is, if I may say it, very unscrupulous."

Lewis became a Christian because the evidence was compelling and inescapable. Even against his will he was "brought in kicking, struggling, resentful, and darting [my] eyes in every direction for a chance of escape." The God "whom I so earnestly desired not to meet" became his Lord and Savior.[26] His book on Christian evidences, *Mere Christianity* (1952), is considered a classic and has been responsible for converting thousands to the faith, including the former skeptic and Watergate-scandal figure, Charles Colson, author of *Born Again* and founder of Prison Fellowship.

Lee Strobel. An award-winning reporter for the *Chicago Tribune* with an MS in law from Yale, he writes,

> For much of my life I was a skeptic. In fact, I considered myself an atheist....I had read just enough philosophy and history to find support for my skepticism....I had a strong motivation to ignore [any problems with skepticism]: a self-serving and immoral lifestyle that I would be compelled to abandon if I were ever to change my views and become a follower of Jesus. As far as I was concerned, the case was closed.[27]

When his beloved wife, Leslie, announced the news she had become a Christian, he was stunned. He undertook a two-year investigation into the facts surrounding the case for Christianity, aided by a hard-boiled reporter's skepticism, training in law, and lots of study:

> Setting aside my self-interest and prejudices as best I could, I read books, interviewed experts, asked questions, analyzed history, explored archaeology, studied ancient literature, and for the first time in my life picked apart the Bible verse by verse...I applied the training I had received at Yale Law School as well as my experience as legal affairs editor of the *Chicago Tribune*. And over time the evidence of the world—of history, of science, of philosophy, of psychology—began to point toward the unthinkable.[28]

After a two-year investigation he found he had to bow before the evidence:

> I see defendants carted off to the death chamber on much less convincing proof! The cumulative facts and data all pointed unmistakably toward a conclusion that I wasn't entirely comfortable in reaching....It would require much more faith for me to maintain my atheism than to trust in Jesus of Nazareth!...In fact, my mind could not conjure up a single explanation that fit the evidence of history nearly as well as the conclusion that Jesus was the one he claimed to be: the one and only Son of God.[29]

Strobel's books—*The Case for Christ: A Journalist's Personal Investigation of the Evidence for Jesus; The Case for Faith: A Journalist Investigates the Toughest Objections to Christianity; God's Outrageous Claims;* and *Inside the Mind of Unchurched Harry and Mary*—are valuable for the inquiring or skeptical mind.

William M. Ramsay. The famous classical scholar and archaeologist Sir William M. Ramsay was once a skeptic of Christianity, convinced that the Bible was fraudulent.

> He regarded the weakest spot in the whole New Testament to be the story of Paul's travels. These had never been thoroughly investigated by one on the spot. So he announced his plan to take the book of Acts as a guide, and by trying to make the same journeys Paul made over the same routes that Paul followed, thus prove that the apostle could never have made them as described....
>
> Equipped as no other man had been, he went to the home of the Bible. Here he spent fifteen years literally "digging for the evidence." Then in 1896 he published a large volume on *Saint Paul the Traveler and the Roman Citizen*.
>
> The book caused a furor of dismay among the skeptics of the world. Its attitude was utterly unexpected, because it was contrary to the announced intention of the author years before. The chagrin and confusion of Bible opponents was complete. But their chagrin and confusion increased, as for twenty years more, book after book from the same author came from the press, each filled with additional evidence of the exact, minute truthfulness of the whole New Testament as tested by the spade on the spot. The evidence was so overwhelming that many infidels announced their repudiation of their former unbelief and accepted Christianity.[30]

Convincing Proofs

Sir William Ramsay's archaeological findings convinced him of the reliability of the Bible and the truth of which it speaks. "Luke's history," he concluded, "is unsurpassed in respect of its trustworthiness"; "Luke is a historian of the first rank....In short, this author should be placed along with the very greatest of historians."[31]

One of the greatest classical scholars of the twentieth century and the outstanding authority on Homer, Dr. John A. Scott, wrote a book at the age of 70, *We Would See Jesus,* concluding a lifetime of mature and ripened convictions. He too was convinced of Luke's veracity: "Luke was not only a doctor and historian, but he was one of the world's greatest men of letters. He wrote the clearest and the best Greek written in that century."

Here we have two of the most able intellects of recent time, among many that could be cited, vouching for the historical accuracy and integrity of Luke, whose Gospel and history (the book of Acts) together comprise one-fourth of the entire New Testament. In Acts 1:3, this able historian declares that Jesus' resurrection had been established "by many convincing proofs."

It is only by means of such convincing proofs that many skeptics such as the above individuals have been led to personal faith in Christ. And the testimonies of these skeptics who have converted to Christianity on the basis of the evidence could be multiplied many times over. The entire *history* of Christianity is checkered with such conversions; in all there are many thousands.

The evidence for Jesus' resurrection, therefore, is more than sufficient to convince even the toughest skeptic who is willing to adjust his or her beliefs on the basis of the biblical and other historical evidence. The wealth of testimony from former skeptics who have converted to Christianity is compelling proof of this.

5

Legal Testimony
About the Resurrection

❧

In the last chapter, we saw that historically the evidence for the resurrection has held up persuasively against intellectual skepticism. But there is still more for the skeptic to consider. From a legal perspective, the evidence is reliable and sufficient to produce a favorable verdict on the resurrection as a historical fact in nearly any modern court of law.

In Acts 1:3, the historian Luke tells us that the resurrected Jesus gave His followers "many convincing proofs that he was alive" (NIV). The Greek for "convincing proofs" is defined in the lexicons as "decisive proof" and indicates the strongest type of legal evidence.[1]

We will assess the evidence as legal testimony concerning the resurrection under the following four points:

1. the legal respectability of the case

2. some specific examples of noted legal testimony

3. the lack of first-century hostile eyewitness reports

4. the overall credibility of the case

The Legal Respectability of the Case for the Resurrection

Lawyers are expertly trained to deal in the matter of evidence; they are taught to sift, weigh, and make valid conclusions as to the nature of the evidence at hand. Skeptics can, if they wish, maintain that only the weak-minded believe in Jesus' literal physical resurrection, but lawyers are not weak-minded. (Nor are the great number of scholars of history, philosophy, literature, science, comparative religion, and theology who have accepted the truth of the resurrection.)[2]

Of course, not every lawyer believes in Jesus' resurrection since belief in Christ is not solely a matter of evidence but also of personal will. But several hundred Christian lawyers are represented by The National Christian Legal Society, The O.W. Coburn School of Law, The Rutherford Institute, Lawyers Christian Fellowship, Trinity International University Law School, Regent University School of Law, and other Christian law organizations, schools, and societies.

> *Logically speaking, virtually every Christian lawyer familiar with the evidence would accept that the resurrection is sufficient to stand up in a court of law.*

Among their number are some of the most respected lawyers in the country, people who have graduated from leading law schools and gone on to prominence in the world of law. For example, among those associated with Trinity International University are Samuel Ericsson, JD, Harvard Law School; Renatus J. Chytil, formerly a lecturer at Cornell and an expert on Czechoslavakian law; John W. Brabner-Smith, Dean Emeritus of the International School of Law, Washington, DC; and Richard Colby, JD, Yale Law

School.[3] All are Christians who accept Jesus' resurrection as historical fact.

Indeed, logically speaking, virtually every Christian lawyer familiar with the evidence would accept that the resurrection is sufficient to stand up in a court of law. Furthermore, as we recount later in this chapter, every trial lawyer we talked to believes that were they to argue the case for the resurrection to a modern jury on the basis of the evidence alone, they could bring in a positive verdict.[4] Thus, the truth of the resurrection can be determined by the very reasoning used in law to determine questions of fact. (This procedure is also true for establishing the historical reliability and accuracy of the New Testament documents.)

William Lane Craig explains the issue as follows:

> If it can be shown that the tomb of Jesus was found empty, that He did appear to His disciples and others after His death, and that the origin of the Christian faith cannot be explained adequately apart from His historical resurrection, then if there is no plausible natural explanation for these facts, one is amply justified in concluding that Jesus really did rise from the dead.
>
> Some modern theologians have objected to this conclusion because it infers from the facts that Jesus rose from the dead, and we are not bound to accept that inference. But not only would such an objection destroy all knowledge of history whatsoever, it would also destroy virtually all knowledge in practical affairs, thus making life impossible. For example, if one day we heard shots from a neighbor's house and saw a man fleeing from the house, and if we found our neighbor dead on the living room floor, and if the police apprehended the fleeing man, and finger-print and ballistics tests showed that he was carrying the murder weapon, then, if these theologians were

correct, we could still not conclude that he shot our neighbor, since this is an inference. But such evidence is accepted in any court of law. The point is that the truth of an inference should be proved beyond any reasonable doubt.

So with the resurrection. If we saw a friend killed and attended his funeral, and if a few days later his grave was found empty and he appeared and spoke to us on several occasions, then, as E.L. Bode remarks in his excellent study on the historical evidence for the empty tomb, the inference that he has been raised to life would not seem to be unwarranted or merely subjective."[5]

Legal Testimony Concerning the Resurrection

In what follows we present a sampling of statements taken from legal experts as to their belief in the factual nature of the resurrection.

Lord Darling, Lord Chief Justice in England during the earlier part of the twentieth century, states, "In its favour as a living truth there exists such overwhelming evidence, positive and negative, factual and circumstantial, that no intelligent jury in the world could fail to bring in a verdict that the resurrection story is true."[6]

Hugo Grotius (1583–1645), a noted "jurist and scholar whose works are of fundamental importance in international law," wrote Latin poetry at the age of eight and entered Leiden University at eleven.[7] Considered "the father of international law," he wrote *The Truth of the Christian Religion* (1627) in which he legally defended the historicity of the resurrection.

J.N.D. Anderson is a scholar of international repute eminently qualified to deal with the subject of evidence. He read law at Cambridge University and has been visiting professor at Princeton University and Harvard Law School. As a leading world authority on Islamic law, he was awarded a doctorate of law from Cambridge for his work in this field. In his work *Christianity: The Witness of History* (1970), he supplies the standard evidences for the resurrection and asks, "How, then, can the fact of the resurrection be denied?" then further emphasizes, "It can be asserted with confidence that men and women disbelieve the Easter story not because of the evidence but in spite of it."[8]

Lionel Luckhoo. The 1990 *Guinness Book of World Records* listed Sir Lionel Luckhoo as the world's most successful lawyer. In his remarkable career, he compiled an unprecedented record of 245 successive murder acquittals. He was also a diplomat of international reputation and was knighted twice by Queen Elizabeth. In his book *The Question Answered: Did Jesus Rise from the Dead?* he wrote, "I have spent more than 42 years as a defense trial lawyer appearing in many parts of the world and am still in active practice. I have just been fortunate to secure a number of successes in jury trials and I say unequivocally the evidence for the resurrection of Jesus Christ is so overwhelming that it compels acceptance by proof which leaves absolutely no room for doubt."[9]

Charles Colson, special counsel lawyer to President Richard M. Nixon, comments on Jesus' disciples in his book *Loving God* (1984), "Take it from one who was inside the Watergate web looking out, who saw firsthand how vulnerable a cover-up is: Nothing less than a witness as awesome as the resurrected Christ could have caused those men to maintain to their dying whispers that Jesus is alive and Lord."[10]

Irwin H. Linton was a Washington, DC, lawyer who argued cases before the U.S. Supreme Court. In his book *A Lawyer Examines the Bible* (1977), he challenges his fellow lawyers "by every acid test known to the law...to examine the case for the Bible just as they would any important matter submitted to their professional attention by a client." He believes that the evidence for Christianity is "overwhelming" and that at least "three independent and converging lines of proof," each of which "is conclusive in itself," establish the truth of the Christian faith. He further asserts that the resurrection "is not only so established that the greatest lawyers have declared it to be the best proved fact of all history, but it is so supported that it is difficult to conceive of any method or line of proof that it lacks which would make [it] more certain."[11]

He also claims,

> There have been many lawyers of this and other days infidel or agnostic. But their legal training gives their views no value unless their attention has seriously been given to a consideration of this matter. And it may safely be believed of all infidel lawyers that no one of them has ever made a careful, lawyer-like, two-sided investigation of the claims of the "Bible and its Christ," studying and digesting any of the great "briefs" or works on the "Christian Evidences" which gather together and sum up the proofs in support of the claim of the Lord Jesus Christ to deity and of the Bible to divine inspiration. I have never found one, and I have hunted for twenty-five years. I have never read of one and I have studied this matter for thirty-five years.[12]

He concludes that the claims of the Christian faith are so well established by such a variety of independent and converging proofs that "it has been said again and again by great lawyers that they cannot but be regarded as proved under the strictest rules of evidence used in the highest American and English courts."[13]

Simon Greenleaf (1783–1853) for 13 years held the Royall Professorship of Law at the Harvard Law School and is the author of the classic three-volume work, *A Treatise on the Law of Evidence* (1842), which "is still considered the greatest single authority on evidence in the entire literature of legal procedure."[14] Perhaps the greatest authority on common-law evidence in Western history, in terms of important legal figures Greenleaf ranks with Sir William Blackstone.

> Greenleaf wrote a volume in which he examined the legal value of the apostles' testimony to the resurrection of Christ. He observed that it was impossible that the apostles "could have persisted in affirming the truths they had narrated, had not Jesus actually risen from the dead, and had they not known this fact as certainly as they knew any other fact."[15]

In his book *An Examination of the Testimony of the Four Evangelists by the Rules of Evidence Administered in the Courts of Justice* (1874), Greenleaf declares,

> All that Christianity asks of men…is, that they would be consistent with themselves; that they would treat its evidences as they treat the evidence of other things; and that they would try and judge its actors and witnesses, as they deal with their fellow men, when testifying to human affairs and actions, in human tribunals.
>
> Let the witnesses [to the resurrection] be compared with themselves, with each other, and with surrounding facts and circumstances; and let their testimony be sifted, as if it were given in a court of justice, on the side

of the adverse party, the witness being subjected to a rigorous cross-examination.

The result, it is confidently believed, will be an undoubting conviction of their integrity, ability and truth.[16]

The Verdict Today

Although admissibility rules vary from state to state and no lawyer can guarantee the decision of any jury (no matter how persuasive the evidence), an abundance of lawyers—a few examples of which follow—testify today that the resurrection would stand in the vast majority of law courts.

John Whitehead, founder of the Rutherford Institute and one of the leading constitutional attorneys defending religious freedom in America, asserts that "the evidence for the resurrection, if competently presented, would likely be affirmed in a modern law court."[17]

Richard F. Duncan, a nationally acclaimed legal scholar whose specialty is constitutional law, graduated from Cornell Law School, practiced corporate law, and has taught at such law schools as Notre Dame, New York University, and the University of Nebraska. He has also written briefs at the Supreme Court level and is the author of a standard work on commercial law, *The Law in Practice of Secure Transaction* (1987). He comments,

> G. Gordon Liddy, who became a Christian some years after serving a prison sentence for Watergate crimes, has described his conversion experience as a "rush of reason." Like Liddy, the legal mind is rational; it seeks persuasive facts and logical conclusions. The resurrection of Jesus Christ, the central fact

of world history, withstands rational analysis precisely because the evidence is so persuasive. The empty tomb, the eyewitness testimony of so many men and women of character who saw the resurrected Christ, and the unblemished integrity of Jesus himself and his claims of deity, all point with inexorable logic to a clear verdict—he has risen. I am convinced this verdict would stand in nearly any modern court of law.[18]

William Burns Lawless, a retired justice of the New York Supreme Court and former dean of Notre Dame Law School, asserted several years ago, "When Professor Simon Greenleaf of Harvard Law School published his distinguished *A Treatise on the Law of Evidence* in 1842, he analyzed the Resurrection accounts in the Gospels. Under the rules of evidence then he concluded a Court would admit these accounts and consider their contents reliable. In my opinion that conclusion is as valid in 1995 as it was in 1842."[19]

Larry L. Crain is a graduate of Vanderbilt University, a general partner in a Tennessee law firm, a member of the United States Supreme Court Bar, the Federal Bar Association, and the American Trial Lawyers Association, and has argued before the Supreme Court. He has told us he agrees in principle with the statement in the previous paragraph.

Not Just Lawyers

And as we have already noted, credible testimony is not limited to merely the field of law—eminent philosophers, historians, scientists, physicians, theologians, and experts in literature and comparative religion can also be cited in abundance, proving that Jesus' resurrection is something to be seriously considered by any thinking person.[20]

Even committed members of a completely different religion will occasionally acknowledge the historical truth of Jesus' resurrection. For instance, noted Jewish theologian Pinchas Lapide, in his book *The Resurrection of Jesus: A Jewish Perspective* (1983), argues for a critical examination of the documentary evidence. Although he denies Jesus' messiahship and rejects the empty tomb as a later apologetic embellishment, he nevertheless concludes: "According to my opinion, the resurrection belongs to the category of the truly real and effective occurrences.... [It is] a fact of history."[21]

Lapide asserts that "if the defeated and depressed group of disciples overnight could change into a victorious movement of faith, based only on autosuggestion or self-deception...then this would be a much greater miracle than the resurrection itself." Further, citing Jewish historical data, he concludes that "the bodily resurrection of a crucified Jew also would not be inconceivable."[22]

He finds it arrogant to suggest that the faith of Christians rests on a falsification, an error, or "a figment of the imagination of a handful of Jews from Galilee"; without the resurrection, "how can one avoid the implication that the churches altogether are based on fraud or self deception?" He concludes,

> As is well known, the church stands and falls with the resurrection of Jesus from the dead....The fact is incontrovertible that the world church which was founded in the name of Jesus originated out of his death....Without the resurrection of Jesus, after Golgotha, there would not have been any Christianity.[23]

The Lack of First-Century Hostile Eyewitness Reports

As a background to the credibility of the resurrection evidence, we should consider the lack of *negative* evidence. The details reported in the Gospels were widely circulated among the early believers both orally and in written form (see, for example, Luke 1:1-2). The apostles' preaching had all but turned Jerusalem upside down (Acts 2:41,47; 6:7; see John 12:19). And their enemies were everywhere. If the events were merely stories thought up by sincere but deluded men, where are the written responses of hostile eyewitnesses who could have set the record straight? Such critics could hardly have remained silent. However,

> out of the first century AD, when the resurrection, if untrue, could have been easily disproved by anyone who took the trouble to talk with those who had been present in Jerusalem during the Passover week of [the year] 33, *no contrary historical evidence has come;* instead, during that century the number of conversions to Christianity increased by geometric progression, the influence of the Gospel story spreading out of Jerusalem like a gigantic web. If Christ did not rise as he promised, how can we rationally explain this lack of negative evidence and number of conversions?[24]

No known record exists of the enemies of Christianity offering any evidence to refute the apostles' claims. Given the magnitude of the claims, this is startling. It appears that critics had no reliable evidence to the contrary; otherwise it would have been offered. The most likely people to attempt a refutation were the Jews who rejected Jesus as their Messiah, yet for the first 200 years they made no attempt (other than Matthew 28:13) to refute the resurrection. And even then, no evidence was offered, merely ad hominem arguments (for example, Jesus was illegitimate, practiced sorcery, and so on). Thus, for the first two centuries AD, even Judaism did not deny Jesus' miracles; they merely believed He performed them through

Satan's power. And for the ensuing 1,800 years there has existed a remarkable "silence" about Jesus.[25] Why?

Does it mean that, in the AD 30s, the evidence for Jesus' resurrection was so persuasive that even the most ardent critic could not dispute it? What other plausible option could explain this silence? We need only to read other writings of that period to realize that critics of many persuasions were publishing refutations, arguments, and counterarguments concerning any number of topics under dispute—but *not* concerning the apostles' testimony about the resurrection.

The Credibility of the Case

> When once the evidence for the empty tomb is allowed to be adequate, the impossibility of any other explanation than that indicated in the New Testament is at once seen. The evidence must be accounted for and adequately explained.[26]

In light of the evidence, unbelief is too great a burden to carry. This is the very reason why throughout history skeptics, in attempting to disprove the resurrection, have frequently been converted to faith in it. As theologian Clark Pinnock asserts, "The resurrection is a fact of history without which history does not make sense."

He continues,

> The resurrection is the only hypothesis which will make peace with all the facts. It constitutes excellent motivation for trusting Christ. Its evidence is sufficiently impressive to demand an answer from every non-Christian. The documentary evidence is superb. Few facts enjoy such corroboration. The resurrection stands within the realm of historical factuality.[27]

In view of the credible evidence, something of this magnitude is certainly worth personal investigation (see Acts 17:30-31). After all, when this unique event is confirmed, it proves that God does exist, that He is a particular *kind* of God, and that He requires a certain kind of response from human beings. If Jesus' resurrection is true, it impacts the eternal destiny of the entire human race.

How important is it for people to personally examine the evidence for the resurrection? Consider an illustration. Suppose that on the day of the Indianapolis 500, the builders of one of the cars come to the track to tell its driver that, unless the car is carefully checked and repaired, there is a 50–50 chance the vehicle will explode by the tenth lap, killing the driver and perhaps others.

> *When our life may be at stake, we…listen carefully to credible sources of information.*

Would the driver be reckless enough to laugh at such a warning? Would he be so foolish as to ignore the builder of his own car and enter the race without checking it? No sensible driver would do this. The builder has *credibility*—more than enough credibility to cause the driver to inspect the car. When our life may be at stake, we too listen carefully to credible sources of information.

But the skeptic who doubts the resurrection merely because of his own philosophical assumptions is making a decision equivalent to driving the race car unchecked. The credibility of the resurrection is established by historical facts, and a person who dismisses them lightly or refuses to even examine them places his or her eternal destiny in jeopardy. God, as the "builder," has provided credible information through history and in other ways.

Author Michael Murphy puts it this way:

> The claim we are investigating for truth-value is not
> only that the God of interstellar space has entered
> our world in the person of Jesus Christ, but that our
> own identity and destiny are contingent upon our
> attitude toward that Person and toward the Truth
> which He proclaimed and manifested. We our-
> selves—and not merely the truth-claims—are at stake
> in the investigation.[28]

And the stakes are high—as high as one's destiny in heaven or
hell.

The world's skeptics, of course, could have gotten rid of
Christianity a long time ago merely by disproving the resurrection. "Once disprove it, and you have disposed of Christianity"[29] as Michael Green notes. But 2,000 years have passed
and Jesus' resurrection still stands. (This means it always will.)
Indeed, at the very time when it could most easily have been
disposed of were it false—the first few days and weeks after
public claims were being circulated—the greatest evidence for
it was established: Jesus' post-resurrection appearances empiri-
cally confirmed it. The disciples were changed forever, none of
their enemies could disprove it, and the church was established.

No Reasonable Alternative

Since the time of Jesus' resurrection, no alternate critical
theories have adequately explained the historical facts as we
have reviewed them:

1. Jesus' resurrection was witnessed by many people.

2. Some of the greatest minds have failed to provide any
   plausible or reasonable re-explanation of the evidence.

The alternate theories (such as the swoon, stolen body, hallucination, mistaken identity, wrong tomb, and so on*) are more difficult to believe than what the New Testament literally and unanimously teaches.

3. Historically, many skeptics who have set out to disprove the resurrection have ended up converting to the Christian faith.

4. Many lines of positive evidence and the lack of negative evidence support a bodily resurrection.

5. The very time it would have been easiest to disprove the resurrection, had it been false, was the very time the greatest evidence for it surfaced.

6. Critics' antisupernatural premises (that is, that miracles never occur) have not proven the resurrection to be false; rather, the historical fact of the resurrection has proved the falsehood of critics' premises.

In addition, the words of some of the greatest legal minds of the modern era concerning the credibility of the resurrection are weighty: namely, the evidence is overwhelming, conclusive, and has never broken down; no historical incident is better or more variously supported; it is a fact beyond dispute, the best-proved fact of history.

The non-Christian reader may well feel that these statements are just the kind one would expect Christians to make. But many who have made them were once skeptics as well. Who could surpass the vigorous intellectual skepticism of William Ramsay or C.S. Lewis, for instance? Few indeed. But at issue here is not who makes such statements but the *evidence* upon which they are made. Besides, even some who remain non-Christian, as we have noted, have admitted that the historical evidence supports the resurrection.

---

* See further our discussion of these theories in appendix B.

The great Princeton theologian Benjamin B. Warfield sketches the skeptic's dilemma:

> It is more impossible that the laws of testimony should be so far set aside, that such witness should be mistaken, than that the laws of nature should be so far set aside that a man should rise from the dead...It is admitted well nigh universally that the Gospels contain testimony for the resurrection of Christ, which, if it stands, proves that fact; and that if Christ rose from the dead all motive for, and all possibility of, denial of any supernatural fact of Christianity is forever removed....
>
> Taking all lines of proof together, it is by no means extravagant to assert that no fact in the history of the world is so well authenticated as the fact of Christ's resurrection. And that established, all Christianity is established too.[30]

Brilliant author and journalist Malcolm Muggeridge puts the situation in a similar light:

> That the resurrection happened...seems to be indubitably true. Likewise, Jesus claimed to be the Light of the World, and [spoke the] related promise that through him we may be reborn into new men, liberated from servitude to the ego and our appetites into the glorious liberty of the children of God. Compared with these tremendous certainties, dubieties about the precise circumstances of Jesus' birth, ministry, death on the cross and continuing presence in the world, seem sterile and unprofitable.
>
> Either Jesus never was or he still is. As a typical product of these confused times, with a skeptical mind and a sensual disposition, diffidently and

unworthily, but with the utmost certainty, I assert that he still is.[31]

Tremendous spiritual realities depend on whether Jesus' bodily resurrection occurred. The evidence for it is compelling—and you, the reader, should consider acting upon that evidence. If you are a believer, it comforts and strengthens your faith; if you are an unbeliever, it challenges you to accept Christianity. Thousands of people before you were once skeptical or indifferent to the resurrection, but then turned to Christ because of the evidence. What do you say?

PART II

QUESTIONS ABOUT THE RESURRECTION ACCOUNTS

The credit due to the testimony of witnesses depends upon, firstly, their honesty; secondly, their ability; thirdly, their number and the consistency of their testimony; fourthly, the conformity of their testimony with experience; and fifthly, the coincidence of their testimony with collateral circumstances.

THOMAS STARKIE

W<small>HY IS IT IMPORTANT FOR US</small> to be aware of alleged contradictions in the accounts of the resurrection and the fact they can be resolved by giving careful attention to the text? Because too many of us have taken for granted the claims of critics that the resurrection accounts conflict, are thus unreliable, and therefore the resurrection itself is questionable or cannot be believed.

To prove that the accounts do not conflict gives evidence of the care and historical accuracy of those who wrote them. And if the Gospel writers were careful historical reporters, then what they say can be trusted—and what they say forms the primary basis of evidence for the resurrection.

If the resurrection of Jesus Christ literally happened, then it is the single most important event in all of human history—as we have already seen in part 1. The integrity of the documents is paramount. So we must ask, do the four resurrection narratives of the Gospels of Matthew, Mark, Luke, and John in any way contradict each other? Do they reflect accurate, independent historical reporting that contains no contradiction or error?

In part 2 we will analyze this crucial issue: whether the separate Gospel accounts are compatible with each other, and whether they thus form reliable eyewitness testimony to the bodily resurrection of Jesus Christ.

6

CONFLICTS IN THE DESCRIPTIONS OF JESUS' DEATH?

⊰❈⊱

*T*HE FIRST CLUSTER OF ALLEGED CONTRADICTIONS has to do with the events leading up to the resurrection. When we compare the four accounts, numerous apparent discrepancies arise in the descriptions of Jesus' crucifixion, death, and burial.

The Crucifixion of Jesus

Who carried Jesus' cross—Simon the Cyrene or Jesus Himself? The synoptic Gospels (Matthew, Mark, and Luke) report the following: "As they led [Jesus] away, they seized Simon from Cyrene, who was on his way in from the country, and put the cross on him and made him carry it behind Jesus" (Luke 23:26, also Matthew 27:32; Mark 15:21). But John seems to suggest that Jesus carried it the whole way Himself: "Carrying his own cross, he went out to the place of the Skull (which in Aramaic is called Golgotha)" (John 19:17).

Because of the beatings and other sufferings following His trials, Jesus was in all probability now extremely weak. A reasonable solution to this apparent contradiction is that Jesus was able to carry the cross only part of the way (John); Simon the Cyrene then carried it the remainder of the way (Matthew, Mark, Luke). It is also possible that Jesus carried part of the cross all of the way while Simon carried the other piece.[1]

Did Jesus drink from the wine mixture given to Him on the cross, or did He refuse it?

- Matthew says He tasted the mixture but refused to drink it (27:34)

- Mark says He was offered the wine but did not take it (15:23)

- Luke mentions only that He was offered wine vinegar (23:36)

- John says that Jesus "received the drink," implying He drank it (19:29-30).

Furthermore, Matthew says the wine was mixed with gall; Mark says it was mixed with myrrh; and Luke and John say it was mixed with vinegar.

We should remember that Jesus was alive on the cross for some six hours. The crucifixion accounts make it clear that on three *separate* occasions a wine mixture was offered to Him. The first offer, as recorded in Matthew and Mark, was made by the soldiers *before* Jesus was crucified. This drink contained wine mixed with "gall" or "myrrh." Customarily it was offered to condemned prisoners as a mild analgesic just prior to cruci-fixion to lessen the pain. But Jesus *refused* that drink (Matthew 27:34; Mark 15:23).

Luke records a second offer by the soldiers to Jesus *after* He was crucified (23:36), this time of wine vinegar or sour wine, a common drink. No mention, however, is made of whether He accepted it.

The third offer, in this instance of wine vinegar, was made to Jesus *shortly before* His death. It occurred after He had uttered the phrase, "My God, my God, why have you forsaken me?" Matthew, Mark, and John mention it, and all three agree that Jesus *accepted the drink* (John 19:28-30; Matthew 27:48; Mark 15:36). A careful reading of the text reveals no contradiction.

What did the inscription placed above Jesus on the cross read?

- Matthew has "This is Jesus, The King of the Jews" (27:37)

- Mark has "The King of the Jews" (15:25)

- Luke has "This is the King of the Jews" (23:38)

- John has "Jesus of Nazareth, The King of the Jews" (19:19)

All four writers mention that the sign included "The King of the Jews"—with Matthew adding "This is Jesus" and John adding "Jesus of Nazareth." In its entirety, the sign probably read "This is Jesus of Nazareth, the King of the Jews." The Gospel writers' piecemeal use of the sign, however, presents no contradiction; each author cites it as best suits his purpose. To do this is not to mislead.

For instance, in a 1964 concert where the Beatles were performing, a large banner was placed across the stage. It read, "The Beatles, the Fabulous Four from London—John, Paul, George, Ringo." Later, writing about the concert, four different reporters could easily have referred to this sign and correctly given four different accounts of what it said without being contradictory. This is precisely what the Gospel writers did.

Did both thieves insult Jesus, or only one of them? Matthew and Mark mention that both thieves insulted Jesus (Matthew 27:44; Mark 15:32), whereas Luke has only one insulting Him (23:39-40). John does not mention the incident.

In resolving this apparent contradiction, we again need to remember that Jesus was alive on the cross for about six hours. It is perfectly reasonable to think both criminals initially insulted Jesus, but as the time passed, one of them, after observing Jesus and listening to Him, changed his mind and later rebuked the other criminal for his insults.

The Death of Jesus

What were Jesus' last words on the cross? If one does not read the texts carefully, it would appear that Matthew and Mark assert that Jesus' last cry was, "My God, my God, why have you forsaken me?" (Matthew 27:46; Mark 15:34). But shortly after this statement, both authors also record that Jesus "cried out again in a loud voice" and then breathed His last ("gave up his spirit") (Matthew 27:50; Mark 15:37).

In other words, both Matthew and Mark refer to a yet later saying of Jesus although they do not identify the words spoken. Luke identifies this loud cry as, "Father, into your hands I commit my spirit" (23:46). John informs us that Jesus uttered, "It is finished" (19:30), though he does not say that Jesus spoke this in a loud voice; thus it presumably immediately preceded Jesus' last words as mentioned by Luke.

What this means is that after Jesus had cried out, "My God, my God, why have you forsaken me?" a brief period of time elapsed. Then, during the last minutes of His life, He uttered, "It is finished," and immediately after that, loudly cried, "Father, into your hands I commit my spirit." At this point, He died. This is not the only possible reconstruction, but it perfectly harmonizes the Gospel evidence. One author adds a saying another leaves out, but this is only to be expected from independent reporting as opposed to collusion.

What did the centurion say when he saw Jesus die?

- Matthew says that after seeing the earthquake and all the amazing events, the centurion and those with him guarding Jesus stated, "Surely he was the Son of God!" (27:54)

- Mark says that when the centurion heard Jesus' last cry and "saw how he died," he exclaimed, "Surely this man was the Son of God!" (15:39)

- Luke records the centurion as saying, "Surely this was a righteous man" (23:47)

- John does not mention the event

It is reasonable to assume, given the miraculous events recorded by Matthew (27:51-54), that the centurion and others guarding Jesus, as well as the many observers, would have known something extremely unusual was happening. In fact, Matthew records in verse 54 that they "were terrified." It is perfectly reasonable, therefore, that both the centurion and those guarding Jesus agreed among themselves that "surely he was the Son of God," with the centurion adding, "surely this was a righteous man." (Luke's rendering may also represent his restatement of the centurion's comment, as preserved in Matthew and Mark, to highlight its implicit meaning concerning Jesus' innocence.) In either event, the sayings do not conflict.

Did "some" women (Mark) or "many" women (Matthew) watch Jesus die?

- Matthew mentions "many" (27:55)

- Mark mentions "some" (15:40)

- Luke merely reports "women" (23:27)
- John does not record the incident

A careful reading of the accounts removes the appearance of contradiction. The synoptic writers record two facts: 1) many people were there, including many women; and 2) some women in this crowd were important to single out because they, as Mark especially details, "had followed [Jesus] and cared for his needs" (15:41; see also Matthew 27:55). But besides emphasizing this select group of women, all three writers point out that many other women were also present at the cross.

The Burial of Jesus

Who took Jesus' body from the cross and buried it—Joseph, or Joseph and Nicodemus? The synoptic Gospels mention that Joseph took and wrapped the body and placed it in the tomb (Matthew 27:59-60; Mark 15:46; Luke 23:53); John, however, has that it was both Joseph and Nicodemus (19:39).

But this phenomenon poses no contradiction. John merely mentions an additional fact that the synoptic writers leave out. The truth of the matter is that Joseph could not have taken the body off the cross and placed it in his tomb all by himself; he would have required the assistance of another individual, whom John identifies as Nicodemus.

Nicodemus's participation in Jesus' burial adds another key witness to these crucial events.

Nicodemus, moreover, plays no visible part in the earlier chapters of the synoptic Gospels, which thus presents no compelling reason to mention him here. But as is well known from

John's Gospel, Nicodemus has a nighttime encounter with Jesus (chapter 3) and represents another important eyewitness to His life, death, and burial, to whom John draws special attention. His participation in Jesus' burial adds another key witness to these crucial events.

Why did only Matthew mention the guard at the tomb?
Many critics have a problem with Matthew's record of the guards at the tomb, probably because their presence there is such powerful testimony to the resurrection of Jesus Christ.* Even though there are no objective grounds for doing so, the account is often summarily dismissed as false. For example, in the 1969 book *The Passover Plot,* Hugh Schonfield claims, "We may dismiss the story in Matthew alone that the chief priests requested to Pilate that a guard be set over the tomb, and that they posted a watch, presumably on Saturday evening at the end of the Sabbath."[2]

Another critic states, "The general scholarly conclusion [is] that the author of Matthew invented the details about the watchful guards, perhaps in hopes of influencing contemporaries who would charge, 'His disciples came by night and stole him away.'"[3]

No basis exists for anyone to completely dismiss an entire event merely because only one trustworthy person mentions it. For instance, if your pastor recalls a personal incident during a Sunday morning message—an incident that could be verified by a number of his friends and acquaintances—do you immediately think he is lying because only he reports it? Further, only Matthew and Luke mention the Sermon on the Mount. Does anyone doubt that Jesus actually preached it merely on the grounds that Mark and John do not mention it?

---

* See further our discussion of the Roman guard placed at the tomb on pages 45–48.

Critics have never been able to supply credible evidence or reasons for throwing out Matthew's testimony concerning the guard. Since he was writing for a Jewish audience, it would be perfectly consistent with his purpose to include an account of Jewish actions. Furthermore, Matthew's account of the guards (27:62-66; 28:11-15) involves 10 verses, or some 15 lines of material—almost half of his resurrection narrative. It seems highly improbable that he would have made up a story that plays so important a part in his account. It could easily have been proven false. But no evidence has been found to suggest that it ever was.

All that is required for the episode to be legitimate is one truthful eyewitness to tell us that the guards were there. Matthew was that eyewitness. But additional historical evidence also supports that a Roman guard was at the tomb. Matthew is not the sole reporter. In the second century, Justin and Tertullian mention it, as do two apocryphal gospels, *The Gospel of the Hebrews* and *The Gospel of Peter*.[4] Further, the Roman governor Pilate would have been inclined "to listen seriously to suggestions by the chief priests on matters of security."[5] Among other reasons, he did not want an uprising of Jesus' followers that could have led to his losing his position as governor of Judea.

There can be no doubt that a Roman guard was actually posted to protect the tomb from thieves. (Certainly guards would never have been posted to protect an empty tomb.) Once they were at their station, they would have done their utmost to make certain the object they were to guard remained there.

The four Gospel accounts of Jesus' crucifixion, death, and burial present no insurmountable obstacles. Plausible reconstructions sensibly resolve the apparent incongruities stemming from a comparison of the four accounts. Rather than contradicting each other, the accounts actually complement one another.

CONFUSION OVER THE FIRST VISITORS TO THE TOMB?

FOUR SPECIFIC QUESTIONS are at issue in regard to the first visitors to the tomb:

1. How many women visited the tomb?

2. Who visited the tomb first?

3. When was the tomb visited?

4. Who supplied the spices to anoint Jesus' body, and when did this take place?

How Many Women Visited the Tomb?

Do the four resurrection narratives contradict each other on the number of women who went to Jesus' tomb?

- Matthew mentions *two* women—Mary Magdalene and the other Mary (28:1)

- Mark mentions *three* women—Mary Magdalene, Mary the mother of James, and Salome (16:1)

- Luke *does not specify a number* but simply mentions "the women" (24:1)

- John mentions *one* woman, Mary Magdalene (20:1)

We must keep in mind that writers have every right to select certain facts according to their literary purposes. To do this does not necessarily misrepresent the historical evidence. We cannot know all the reasons why one author selects information that another does not. It would make a writer's job virtually impossible if he or she had to list all the reasons for including certain details and omitting others.

Mark feels it is important, for some reason, to report that Salome was at the tomb, while Matthew does not. Perhaps Salome was the woman, or one of several women, who recounted the events to Mark. Perhaps Matthew does not mention Salome because he documented the event from a source that did not include her.

Some critics charge that Luke disagrees with Matthew and Mark because he mentions only "the women." But this argument is without force. None of the Gospel writers say it was *only* two women, or *only* one woman, or *only* three women. Each writer mentions those he wants to recognize—perhaps according to special literary emphases or because this is all the information he presently knows or can readily substantiate. *But none of them give contradictory information.* If one of the four writers had said *only* so-and-so went to the tomb, and another had said *only* somebody else went, then we would have a contradiction.

In referring merely to "the women," Luke does not contradict Matthew and Mark; he merely is less specific. However, does John contradict the other three writers because he records only one woman, Mary Magdalene, going to the tomb? Two perfectly reasonable explanations present themselves here.

First, all the women may have set out for the tomb, with Mary arriving first. John simply records the earliest arrival. Or second, John may have chosen to write only about Mary, even though he could have written about all of them. These possibilities are, of course, not mutually exclusive.

As with the other writers, John does not say that *only* Mary Magdalene went to the tomb. But he is perfectly free to concentrate on Mary Magdalene, especially if her experience is important to his writing interests. He probably features her for a number of reasons: 1) After the resurrection, Jesus appeared to her first (and not to one of the disciples; see Mark's appendix, 16:9); 2) Mary looked into the tomb and saw the two angels (John 20:11-12); 3) Mary personally met the resurrected Jesus near the empty tomb (verses 11-18); and 4) Jesus commissioned her to go and tell the disciples the good news (verse 17).

Different Sources

We must also keep in mind that each of the writers may have derived their information from different sources. Luke, for example, records, "It was Mary Magdalene, Joanna, Mary the mother of James, and the others with them who told this [about the empty tomb and the angels' message] to the apostles" (Luke 24:10).

Picture the different women, immediately after their dramatic encounter with the angels, each bursting with explanations of what they had seen and thought was important to tell the disciples who happened to be standing near them right then. This may also explain why certain facts are mentioned and others omitted. The listeners may have heard bits from each of the women, most of it from just one, or most of it from several.

In *The Easter Enigma,* John Wenham suggests that "Luke's is a straightforward account written from Joanna's point of view* (Luke 8:3; 24:10), whereas Mark's is an account written from the point of view of the other three women."[1] Similarly, John may have written his version strictly from Mary Magdalene's viewpoint, assuming that the majority of Christians had already known that this group of women went to the tomb. Perhaps he decided to share additional details of what had happened to Mary Magdalene because it was less familiar to his readers.

Indeed, when Luke mentions "the others with them" (24:10), we could even assume that more than three women were present at the tomb on Easter morning. If Luke is describing the women who actually visited the tomb, then there were at least five—Joanna and "the others" signifies at least one more person than Salome. It is also possible that the "other women" to whom Luke alludes were part of the group who reported to the disciples.

To sum up, we know that at least three women visited the tomb, and possibly more. The resurrection accounts are not contradictory. None of the writers state that only a set number of women visited the tomb. Rather, each selected details from a broader pool of evidence according to his purpose in writing.

Who Visited the Tomb First?

As we noted earlier, John may have concentrated on documenting Mary Magdalene's visit to the tomb either 1) to the exclusion of the other women, or 2) because she was probably the first person to arrive at the tomb. The second option is preferable. It is quite possible that all the women had planned to meet at the tomb and left their homes at approximately the same time. Mary arrived first, observed the empty tomb, and

---

* Joanna was a wealthy supporter of Jesus, whose husband was "steward" to Herod Antipas, ruler of Galilee.

before her companions arrived, ran to tell Peter and John about it. Thus, Matthew, Mark, and Luke could talk generally about all the women going to the tomb—and they would be correct; John could report specifically that Mary reached the tomb first—and he would be correct.

This reconstruction of the event would explain John's account as it stands. The other Gospel accounts would also permit it, especially Mark and Matthew, which at this juncture have unannounced breaks in their resurrection narratives. These occur between Mark 16:1 and 16:2 and between Matthew 28:1 and 28:2 and again between verses 4 and 5.* These breaks allow for the possibility that Mary came first to the tomb and that the "other women" arrived shortly after she left. Furthermore, Luke's inclusion of Mary with the "other women" who report to the disciples what happened at the tomb (Luke 24:9-11) does not conflict with this.†

But there is at least one more plausible reconstruction as well: that Mary arrived at the tomb first while it was still dark and was still there when the other women arrived. In essence, all the women mentioned by the Gospel writers, as a group, arrived at the tomb at about the same time.[2] Whichever of these reconstructions one prefers, neither of them poses contradictions for the resurrection accounts.

When Was the Tomb Visited?

The specific *time* the women went to the tomb has also been called into question. Matthew says "at dawn" (Matthew 28:1), while Mark has "just after sunrise" (Mark 16:2). But here, too, the objection is flimsy.

An announcement of an Easter "sunrise" service nicely illustrates this. One reporter might state that the service begins

---

* For further discussion of this abbreviated writing style, see pages 141–142.

† For a probable chronological sequence of events here, see that offered by Norval Geldenhuys, *Commentary on the Gospel of Luke* (Grand Rapids, MI: Eerdmans, 1975), pp. 626–628, also cited in full on pages 160–163 of this book.

"at dawn," while another says "just after sunrise." As we know, "at dawn" includes "just after sunrise." If today's writers frequently do not use precise time language, why should we expect it of the Gospel authors? Both phrases, "at dawn" and "just after sunrise," can involve a significant span of time. If we say we went to the beach "at dawn," the hearer understands that we could mean anything from some minutes before sunrise to some minutes after. It is similarly the case for Matthew and Mark.

Next, Luke is thought to disagree with Matthew and Mark because he has "very early in the morning" (Luke 24:1). Again, though, this time expression is similar to, if not synonymous with, those given in Matthew and Mark. In fact, the phrase could refer to anytime after midnight! "Very early in the morning" encompasses a sizeable portion of time. Luke's rendering is, therefore, compatible with Matthew and Mark.

But doesn't John most definitely have a contradiction? His phrase "while it was still dark" (John 20:1), many say, is certainly not compatible with "at dawn" or "just after sunrise," when obviously it would no longer be dark. But we must consider again the normal use of language. "While it was still dark" *can* describe conditions that exist "at dawn."

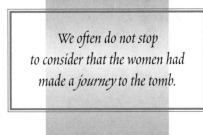

We often do not stop to consider that the women had made a journey to the tomb.

Everyone who has been up "at dawn" certainly knows it is not yet fully light. In fact, depending on weather conditions, it can be quite dark even "at dawn" or "just after sunrise."

In addition, other factors indicate that there is no contradiction among the accounts. The writers may have had in mind different periods of time; the starting point could have been when the women left their houses, were traveling, or actually arrived at the tomb. Examining the Greek, Bible scholar Gleason Archer suggests that the women

> "apparently started their journey from the house in Jerusalem while it was still dark...even though it was already early morning... (John 20:1). But by the time they arrived, dawn was glimmering in the East.... Mark 16:2 adds that the tip of the sun had actually appeared above the horizon.[3]

We often do not stop to consider that the women had made a *journey* to the tomb. Where the women were in each author's mind when he starts his account of their trip to the tomb would influence the kind of time language he uses. No real grounds for a contradiction arise here.

There is an additional reason why the time expressions in the four accounts may differ: certain of the women made a delay to purchase spices (presuming that they acquired them Sunday morning rather than the evening before, after the sabbath was over). This would have required additional time and would explain the difference between John's Gospel and the others. In this event, Mary herself would have arrived at the tomb alone, before the other women.[4]

John Wenham takes a step further and simply suggests there is no cause to find a contradiction here:

> There is perhaps no need to insist upon any distinction between Matthew's "toward the dawn," Mark's "very early," Luke's "early dawn" and John's "while it was still dark." Darkness and light are relative terms and it would be perfectly possible, and not inaccurate, for one person to describe the time as "early dawn" which another described as "still dark." It needs to be

remembered, however, that it could have been undeniably dark on the women's departure and undeniably
light on their arrival, particularly if their starting-
point were Bethany....We undoubtedly get a consistent and coherent picture if we see the first departures
as being in the dark and the last arrivals as being
before [full] sunrise.[5]

Who Supplied the Spices to Anoint Jesus' Body, and When Was the Anointing Done?

John records that on Friday evening, before the sabbath
began, "Nicodemus brought a mixture of myrrh and aloes,
about seventy-five pounds. Taking Jesus' body, the two of
them [Nicodemus and Joseph of Arimathea] wrapped it, with
the spices, in strips of linen. This was in accordance with
Jewish burial customs" (John 19:39-40).

But according to Luke, certain unnamed women had followed Jesus from Galilee. After seeing His crucifixion, the
tomb where His body was laid, "they went home and prepared
spices and perfumes" (Luke 23:56). They rested on the sabbath, but on Sunday morning brought the spices to the tomb
to anoint Jesus' body (24:1; see also Mark 16:1-2).

According to both Mark and Luke, the women never had
the opportunity to anoint Jesus' body. When they arrived at
the grave, the body was absent—Jesus had already risen.

Why the women wanted to anoint Jesus' body after Joseph
and Nicodemus had already done so is answered by scholar
John Lilly:

> Decent burial according to the standards of the day was
> the most highly cherished and ardently desired lot of
> every Jew; its privation was deemed a frightful misfor-
> tune. Relatives and friends of the deceased considered

it a grave obligation to discharge this office on behalf of
their departed.[6]

In view of this, the women most likely felt that in the rush
to move Jesus' body after the crucifixion, it had not been properly prepared before the sabbath had started. The women's
desire to anoint Jesus' body a second time poses, therefore, no
error or contradiction.

Lastly, only Mark and Luke mention that the women
brought spices, whereas Matthew and John do not mention
this at all. However, all four evangelists would have known
that Jesus' body required anointing according to Jewish burial
customs. It is perfectly reasonable for two to mention it and
two to assume it.

In summary, the evidence suggests that no necessary contradiction exists in the accounts of women who went to the
tomb on Easter morning and the timing of their arrival.

We must remember that the Gospel writers are reporting
these events somewhat independently. The hallmark of independent reporting is differences in content. In a court of law,
for example, it is *always* true that four witnesses describing a
traffic accident (or a crime, or any other incident) will each
supply different information. Witnesses notice and report
those things that are unique, relevant, or important to them.

The same is true for the Gospel writers. Each one devotes
differing amounts of space and detail to the women coming to
the tomb. Matthew and Mark supply eight verses each
(Matthew 28:1-8; Mark 16:1-8); Luke has ten verses (Luke
24:1-10); and John only two (John 20:1-2). Each mention
some details that the others do not.

It is actually more unreasonable to suppose that every Gospel writer would have recorded the event in precisely the same way, giving precisely the same details. This would be evidence of collusion, not independent testimony. There is no reason to demand that the Gospel writers report the same details. When critics charge that contradictions exist merely because the accounts differ, they are being unfair. They are holding the Gospel authors to a standard to which they would not subject themselves.

8

Doubts About the Angels at the Tomb?

⸎

Another set of concerns about the Gospel accounts has to do with the angels at the tomb. These include the following questions:

1. How many angels were at the tomb?
2. Were these beings men or angels?
3. What was their position and location at the tomb?
4. Do Matthew's, Mark's, and Luke's versions of the angel's message to the women at the tomb conflict?
5. Does Luke's reference to Galilee contradict Matthew and Mark?
6. Do Matthew, Mark, and Luke contradict each other in describing the women's reaction to the angel's message?

How Many Angels Were at the Tomb?

An apparent difficulty of the resurrection narratives is that Matthew and Mark refer to *one* angel (Matthew 28:2-4;

Mark 16:5), while Luke and John refer to *two* (Luke 24:5; John 20:12).

Here the principle we emphasized in the last chapter again applies. Although the four Gospel writers deal with the same event, they are not obligated to include every detail known to them or, for that matter, the same details the others record in their accounts.

Mark merely recounts that the women encounter an angel sitting on the right side of the tomb, who proceeds to give them a message. (He compresses the story here as Matthew has done at other places in his resurrection account.) Luke, on the other hand, supplies more details. He states that, in addition to the angel who speaks, a second angel is present. Apparently the second angel remains silent.

> It should be said once and for all that the mention by one evangelist of two angels and by another of one does not constitute a contradiction or discrepancy. If there were two, there was one....Contradiction would only be created if the writer who mentioned the one should go on to say explicitly that there was only one....It needs to be remembered that we are dealing with two *descriptions* of an event, and not with two witnesses replying to cross-examination....These witnesses are not answering the question "How many?"— they are giving (as all descriptions must be) incomplete descriptions of a complex event.[1]

In fact, at Jesus' resurrection, *many* different angels may have been intermittently present at the tomb. Although Matthew, Mark, Luke, and John differ on details concerning the number of angels, their accounts do not contradict. Rather, they are complementary.

Were These Beings Men or Angels?

- Matthew reports "an angel" (28:2)

- Mark describes "a young man" (16:5)

- Luke writes "two men" (24:4)

- John reports "two angels" (20:12)

Do these accounts conflict, or are they confused on this point? Whenever angels appear to people in Scripture, they are almost always said to take the form of men. This is not surprising; it may be deliberate on their part to reduce the anxiety of those with whom they come into contact. But they often eventually reveal their angelic identity in some unique way, as in Matthew 28:2-3; at times they may keep it entirely hidden, as is plain from Hebrews 13:2. Therefore, it is not contradictory for the four Gospel writers to refer to the angels as men or as angels. Both are correct.

Regardless, Matthew and John are specific: Matthew writes, "an angel of the Lord"; John, "two angels in white." Although Luke and Mark describe their appearance as men, Luke clearly identifies them as angels, noting they were "in clothes that gleamed like lightning" (24:4). Even though the Bible frequently describes angels as men,* little doubt usually remains as to their angelic identity. In fact, at times angels are first described as men and later as angels in the very same passage (for example, in Judges 13:2-22). This biblical phenomenon, in all probability, properly explains how Luke and Mark understood the identity of the "men" who appeared to the women at the tomb; and it underscores how important it is to read the resurrection narratives in light of these other parts of Scripture.

---

* For example, Genesis 18:1-22; 19:1-17; Judges 13:2-22; Daniel 10:5,16,18; 12:5-7; Acts 1:10; 10:30; Hebrews 13:2.

What Were the Position and the Location of the Angels at the Tomb?

The issue concerning the location and position of the angels at the tomb is complex and liable to confusion. Critics allege that Matthew has an angel only *outside* the tomb while Mark, Luke, and John have angel(s) *inside* the tomb.

In harmonizing the Gospel accounts, we should keep in mind that if two or more angels were present at various stages of the event, they could have been in a variety of locations and positions inside and outside the tomb. If we first examine Matthew and Mark, then add Luke to the discussion, and end with John, that will help clarify the events.

Does Matthew Conflict with Mark?

In Matthew, the initial location of the angel is outside the tomb. He appears for a specific purpose, both to immobilize the guards and to roll away the stone to let the witnesses in.

Matthew does not mention that this angel subsequently entered the tomb. Thus, reading his narrative only, it seems as if the angel remained outside when he delivered his message to the women (Matthew 28:4-5). Matthew does not supply the information between verses 4 and 5 that the other Gospel writers do—namely, that the angel went inside the tomb and there spoke to the women.

Why did the angel go inside the tomb? Probably for two reasons: so as not to frighten the women, and because this is where they would naturally go after observing that the stone had been rolled back. It seems the angel specifically wanted the women to enter the tomb so they could observe the absence of Jesus' body.

If we consult Mark, we see he clearly states that the women "entered the tomb" and there saw an angel "on the right side" (16:5). Furthermore, Mark recounts that after the women went into the tomb, the angel gave them the same message as recorded in Matthew: "See the place where they laid him" (Mark 16:6; Matthew 28:6).

From this we understand that in Matthew the angel's "request" to "come and see the place where he lay" is not a request for the women outside the tomb to come inside, but to them from within the tomb so they would take special notice of exactly where Jesus' body was placed and that it was no longer there. (Tombs in those days were often large sepulchers the size of small rooms.) Clearly, the angel was outside the tomb at one point. But Matthew never says that the angel permanently remained outside and could not have changed locations at some point to speak to the women.

Ancient accounts and histories "sometimes...incorporated in a single story a number of actions and speeches which had a common theme, not indicating at all the time of the occurrence."

Here it is important to note a literary technique Matthew has used in recording some of the events in his Gospel. The event—the angel appearing at the tomb, the guards being frightened into silence, the women coming to the tomb, and so on—are all compressed. Comparing Matthew with the other Gospel accounts substantiates this. But even though Matthew at times recounts events with no apparent break in time, we are able to determine from other sources that an interval occasionally separates one event from another. (Contemporary writers do the same thing every day.)

Furthermore, ancient accounts and histories

> sometimes...incorporated in a single story a number of
> actions and speeches which had a common theme,

not indicating at all the time of the occurrence. Sometimes they jumped back and forward between two or more parallel sequences of events, leaving it to the reader to understand that each item is as it were a flash on a cinema screen.[2]

Matthew's narrative of the events which took place at the tomb is very likely one such example. As we noted, Matthew makes no record of the angel going into the tomb. But after the angel appeared and silenced the Roman guard, he proceeded into the tomb, as the other Gospels would indicate. It is also highly probable that at this time another angel appeared in the tomb with him.

With this probable scenario between Matthew and Mark in mind, we can now consider what Luke says happened at the tomb.

Does Luke Contradict Matthew and Mark?

Luke records that suddenly two men *stood* beside the women inside the tomb (24:4). Mark's version reports that upon entering the tomb, the women saw an angel "*sitting* on the right side" (16:5). So were two angels standing, or was one angel sitting?

To start with,

> We know too little about the manner of angel appearances to be sure that Luke and John mention the same two angels, or that Matthew and Mark mention the same one....
>
> This suggests the very plausible idea that instead of one or two angels there was probably a whole legion of them present to honor their Lord in his greatest moment of triumph on earth. First one, then another appears in visible form.[3]

We should also keep in mind that, unlike men, angels can make themselves visible or invisible at will.

Moreover, the Greek word for "standing" may clear up much of the problem concerning the angels' position between Mark and Luke. The word Luke uses in 24:4, translated "stood beside," can also be translated "came upon" or "appeared." Luke probably intends to stress the *suddenness* of the angels' appearing, rather than their precise position. Mark tells us only that *when* they appeared they were seated, a position calculated to put the women at ease.

Wenham summarizes these accounts as follows:

> It would seem that there were two angels, one more prominent than the other. They (or he) first lifted the great stone and rolled it from the entrance and then sat upon it until the guards had left. They then retired inside and were invisible when the first women arrived. They made themselves visible to them and delivered their message. When Peter and John arrived they were again invisible [or gone], but they had reappeared when Mary Magdalene looked into the tomb [at her second visit].[4]

Does John's Account Conflict with Matthew, Mark, and Luke?

In John's Gospel the two angels are seated, one at the head and the other at the foot of where Jesus had lain (John 20:12). The two angels speak to Mary from inside the tomb at the stated locations. This seems to indicate a conflict—however, it is wrong to claim this is the *same* event described in Matthew, Mark, and Luke. Why? Because a logical sequence of events suggests otherwise.

John and Mark apparently both agree that Mary Magdalene was the first person to whom Jesus appeared (John 20:14;

Mark 16:9). Yet, according to Mark, Jesus must have appeared to Mary sometime other than when her companions, Mary the mother of James and Salome, came to the tomb early Easter Sunday morning (Mark 16:2). In reading Mark 16:2, it sounds as if Mary was with her companions. But how then could Mark say that Mary Magdalene was the first to see Jesus if her companions were with her (verse 9)? The solution is that Jesus appeared to Mary at her *second* visit to the tomb, not her first.

Mark states that they all came to the tomb early Sunday morning. If we assume that Mary arrived earlier than her companions, Mark's version does not contradict John. Mary probably arrived at the tomb ahead of the others and intended to wait for them there. But after she arrived, she noticed that the stone had been rolled away and the tomb was empty; instead of waiting for the others, she immediately set off to tell Peter and John (John 20:1-2).

Meanwhile, her companions, the other Mary and Salome, arrive at the tomb and the angels appear to them (Mark 16:1). The lead angel tells them to report the good news to the disciples that Jesus has risen from the dead. The women leave. A short time later Peter and John arrive after hearing the news from Mary that the tomb is empty.

Mary follows Peter and John back to the tomb, although she lags behind them—first, because she is tired after running from the tomb to tell the disciples the stunning news; second, because the two disciples themselves are running to the tomb after hearing the news. John even outruns Peter (John 20:2,4).

By the time Mary returns to the tomb, Peter and John have already left (John 20:10). All alone, Mary stands in front of the tomb, begins to cry, and then looks into the tomb, whereupon she sees two angels, one seated where Jesus' head had been, the other where His feet had been. Jesus then appears to her in the garden.

The appearance of the two angels to Mary as recorded by John is entirely different from the event described by the other Gospel writers. Mary's encounter with the angels happened after Peter and John left to go and tell the others what had happened. According to this sequence of events, John's account complements Matthew, Mark, and Luke.

Do Matthew, Mark, and Luke Conflict About the Angel's Message to the Women?

We have solid grounds for believing that, historically, an angel gave a single unified message to the women at the tomb. However, the Gospel writers then included the parts of the message they thought important for their literary purposes. We get portions of it from each of the three evangelists. But we have confidence that these portions of the message are authentic, based on eyewitness testimony that had come down to the writers orally or in written form.

Although the accounts of the angel's message differ somewhat in length and emphasis, they do not contradict each other. Nothing demands that the Gospel writers had to give their readers a word-for-word recounting of the message. Luke retains enough words that agree with Matthew and Mark for us to know that he refers to the same message, though his emphasis differs from the other two writers on his use of the term *Galilee*. But the thrust remains the same: The resurrected Jesus will go before the disciples into Galilee.

To begin, the angel's message as recorded by Matthew and Mark is strikingly similar. Mark, however, includes a specific reference to Peter: "Go, tell [Jesus'] disciples *and Peter,* 'He is going ahead of you into Galilee. There you will see him, just as he told you'" (16:7). But why is Mark the only one who records this? According to reliable Christian tradition from the second century,[5] Mark was Peter's friend and traveling companion.

Most of his Gospel, it is believed, derived from Peter's eyewitness testimony to the events. Therefore, it is natural to find this additional piece of information concerning Peter in Mark's Gospel. Peter apparently conveyed to Mark how wonderful it was that Jesus had had the angel specifically mention that he, Peter (who had denied his Lord), should be told that Jesus had risen and wanted to see him.

But Luke is accused of completely altering the angel's message, even adding to it. For example, according to Luke, the angel asks the women, "Why do you look for the living among the dead?" (Luke 24:5). Still more importantly, Luke adds, "Remember how he told you, while he was still with you in Galilee: 'The Son of Man must be delivered into the hands of sinful men, be crucified and on the third day be raised again'" (verses 6-7). Matthew and Mark mention neither of these messages.

However, the absence of the latter two verses in Matthew and Mark hardly rules out the possibility that the angel indeed said this. All three Gospels unanimously agree that Jesus made such a prediction about Himself on several occasions: for example "The Son of Man is going to be betrayed into the hands of men. They will kill him, and on the third day he will be raised to life" (Matthew 17:22-23).

Mark records, "He began to teach them that the Son of Man must suffer many things and be rejected by the elders, the chief priests and the teachers of the law, and that he must be killed, and after three days rise again" (Mark 8:31). Luke records this as well in 9:22.

Jesus' self-prediction was apparently relatively common in His teaching (see Matthew 16:21; Mark 10:33-34; Luke 18:31-33). Clearly then, this additional message of the angel in Luke 24:6-7 derives from Jesus' actual sayings. Its authenticity is strong even though Matthew and Mark did not mention it in their versions.

Does Luke's Reference to Galilee Contradict Matthew and Mark?

In the first two Gospels the disciples are told to go *to Galilee,* where they will meet the resurrected Jesus. But in Luke the angel does not say that Jesus will appear to them in Galilee, but only that it was *in Galilee* Jesus predicted His resurrection.

Matthew and Mark have the angel quoting the exact words Jesus gave to His disciples earlier. Both state that when He was in Galilee, Jesus said to them, "After I have risen, I will go ahead of you into Galilee" (Matthew 26:32; Mark 14:28).

After the resurrection, according to Matthew, the angel instructs the women, "Go quickly and tell his disciples: 'He has risen from the dead and is going ahead of you into Galilee. There you will see him. Now I have told you'" (Matthew 28:7).

In Mark, the angel says, "Go, tell his disciples and Peter, 'He is going ahead of you into Galilee. There you will see him, just as he told you'" (Mark 16:7).

Luke apparently knows that the angel quotes the prediction Jesus gave to His disciples in Galilee (although he also omits Jesus' giving of the prediction in his Gospel; compare Luke 22:31-34 to Matthew 26:31-34 and Mark 14:27-31). But instead of recording the angel quoting it, Luke simply refers to it and its meaning by reporting the angel as saying, "Remember how he told you while he was still with you in Galilee" (24:6). Thus, in the disciples' act of remembering the prediction, their knowledge would coincide with what Matthew and Mark record: "He has risen from the dead and is going ahead of you into Galilee."

Luke's particular reference to Galilee is probably chiefly because of his particular interest in documenting Jesus' appearances to the disciples in and around Jerusalem (Luke 24:33-53). We need to remember that nothing demands that Luke should have given a word-for-word rendering of what the angel said. He probably knew what had been said concerning Galilee and its importance, and signaled this by referring to it in the angel's message.

But did he give enough information for his readers to understand what was meant? Certainly. He records the angel's message in a way that would enable his readers to recall Jesus' prediction of His death and resurrection, and His promise to meet His disciples in Galilee.

Was Luke wrong, however, in taking the liberty to reword the angel's message to the women? No, all of us do this kind of thing every day.

> We must extend the same courtesy to the biblical authors that we do to modern writers, who select material appropriate to their purposes and edit it as they see fit.

For example, when the *Challenger* Space Shuttle exploded and its crew of seven astronauts died, many of us probably flipped from channel to channel to catch different news accounts of the same terrible event. Different descriptions were given, and even different facts were added or omitted. But such differences didn't lead us to conclude that the accident never happened.

Furthermore, if one of the channels added new information or gave a slightly different emphasis in their report, did we assume that the various news accounts could not be harmonized? Not at all. The same is true for the Gospels. When one writer gives additional information or places his own emphasis on one part of the story, and reasonable attempts at harmonization successfully blend the elements together, no contradiction need be assumed.

Selective reporting is just that: Material selected according to the author's or editor's purpose. For example, the apostle John, omits the angel's message altogether. Are we to assume the event never happened merely because he omitted it? Of course not. The Gospel authors' purpose in writing often heavily influenced what they chose to report and the way they went about doing so.

We must extend the same courtesy to the biblical authors that we do to all writers, who select material appropriate to their purpose and edit it as they see fit. The key is not what the Gospel writers omit, but the truthfulness of what they say.

And from what we have seen, they are truthful. They do not contradict each other in their record of the angel's message. When we fit together the various elements given in the three Gospel accounts, it is fairly easy to reconstruct the original message as probably given by the lead angel:

> Don't you be afraid. I know whom you are seeking—Jesus the Nazarene, the crucified one. Why do you seek the living among the dead? He is not here—for he is risen, as he said. Come, see the place where they laid him. Remember how he talked to you when he was in Galilee, saying that the Son of man must be betrayed into the hands of sinful men and be crucified and on the third day rise. Go quickly, tell his disciples (and Peter) that he is raised from the dead and is going before you into Galilee. You will see him there, as he said.[6]

Each writer has simply selected the part of the angel's message that best suits his purpose.

Do Matthew, Mark, and Luke Contradict Each Other in Describing the Women's Reaction to the Angel's Message?

- Matthew says the women "ran to tell [Jesus'] *disciples*" about the empty tomb (28:8)

- Mark records, however, "They said *nothing to anyone*, because they were afraid" (16:8)

- Furthermore, Luke says, "They told all these things *to the Eleven* and *to all the others*" (24:9)

But does Mark's record of the women's fearful silence necessarily contradict Matthew's or Luke's report that they freely told many people about what they had seen and heard at the tomb? Did the women tell or not?

Once again, when the accounts are fitted together and time is factored in, the discrepancy disappears. At first, before they had reached the disciples, the women said nothing to anyone because they were afraid. Each of us would have been so as well. But we are dealing with a specific period of time (the time it took the women to go from the tomb to the others). Their initial response of fear did not subside until they had a chance to tell the disciples what had happened. Once safely there with them, they could deliver their message to the disciples and then to Jesus' other followers.

The angel's command to the women, "Go tell the disciples," suggests that the disciples should be the first to hear the message. Mark merely emphasizes that the women were scared; in their haste to reach the disciples, they doubtlessly had to "collect themselves" along the way. That they eventually told them is obvious, for the three other Gospels record their reaction to the women's astounding news.*

---

* Mark's somewhat surprising and rather unconventional ending in 16:8 (16:9-20 was probably an appendix added by a later hand) highlights the women's fear and that they presumably said nothing until they reached the disciples.

In summary, the alleged contradictions concerning the angels at the tomb, the message of the angel, and the women's reaction have very plausible solutions supporting the compatibility of the four resurrection narratives. They complement rather than contradict each other. This factor does not show collusion but rather truthfulness in reporting. The writers merely reported the events selectively, as all writers do.

9

Clashes in the Accounts of Jesus' Appearances?

The final cluster of alleged contradictions centers around the resurrection appearances of Jesus. Three questions are especially pertinent here:

- Do Mark and Luke conflict in their accounts of the two disciples on the road to Emmaus?
- Did Jesus appear in Jerusalem or only on a mountain in Galilee?
- Can other discrepancies in the four Gospels concerning Jesus' resurrection appearances be resolved?

Do the Accounts of the Two Disciples on the Road to Emmaus Conflict?

Luke records Jesus' appearance to the two disciples seven miles outside of Jerusalem on the road to Emmaus (24:13-36). According to Luke, they return to Jerusalem to tell the others of their experience, only to discover that those present had already heard the news. They found some of them saying, "It is true! The Lord is risen and has appeared to Simon" (verse 34). The two disciples then go on to tell of their encounter.

However, Mark 16:12-13 reads as follows.* "Jesus appeared in a different form to two of them while they were walking in the country. These returned and reported it to the rest; *but they did not believe them either.*"

Scholars widely accept that the Luke and Mark passages refer to the same event. But an apparent discrepancy surfaces here. Did the Eleven believe the testimony of the two (as Luke seems to suggest) or not (as Mark's appendix plainly asserts)? First, we need to understand that, according to Luke, the people exclaiming, "The Lord has risen and has appeared to Peter," probably included few of the Eleven. These people were among "those with" the Eleven and came to inform them that Jesus was resurrected (Luke 24:33). These select few believed in the resurrection because they had witnessed the risen Jesus first-hand. But most of the others in the room, including many of the Eleven, had not yet seen the risen Jesus and thus still found it difficult to believe what they said.

In carefully examining what Luke says about the events, we see he closely agrees with Mark 16:12-13. After the two men recognized Jesus on the road to Emmaus, "They…returned at once to Jerusalem. There they found the Eleven and *those with them,* assembled together and saying, 'It is true! The Lord has risen and has appeared to Simon'" (Luke 24:33-34).

The key issue in Luke revolves around the identity of "those with" the Eleven (verse 33). This group must have included at least Mary Magdalene, whose report the Eleven had earlier refused to believe (Mark 16:10-11), and probably also the other women who had seen the angel and the resur-rected Lord (Matthew 28:5-10).

---

* Mark's appendix, 16:9-20, is not found in the earliest manuscripts and probably represents a later addi-tion by a Christian copyist.

Luke seems to imply the Eleven were mainly bystanders, listening to those among them who were testifying that Jesus had risen. Nowhere does Luke say that the Eleven actually believed what these people were telling them. Rather, the evidence clearly indicates most of the Eleven did not yet fully believe the resurrection had taken place: While they were gathered together, Jesus Himself suddenly appeared in their midst and rebuked them for *doubting* He had risen. "[The Eleven] were startled and frightened, thinking they saw a ghost" (Luke 24:37). Jesus encouraged them to "Touch me and see; a ghost does not have flesh and bones, as you see I have" (verse 39). And even then "they *still did not believe* it because of joy and amazement" (verse 41).

Mark 16:14 similarly records, "Later Jesus appeared to the Eleven as they were eating; he rebuked them for their *lack of faith* and their *stubborn refusal to believe* those who had seen him after he had risen." The report in Mark's appendix closely corresponds to Luke's account. The passages do not conflict.

Did Jesus Appear in Jerusalem or Only on a Mountain in Galilee?

The New Testament records at least 12 separate appearances of the resurrected Jesus to His followers. "The Gospels profess to give us only a selection of events in the Jesus story (John 21:25) but even so there is an impressive list."[1] He appeared to

1. Mary Magdalene (Mark 16:9; John 20:1-18)
2. the two Marys (Matthew 28:1-10)
3. Simon Peter (Luke 24:34; 1 Corinthians 15:5)
4. the disciples on the road to Emmaus (Luke 24:13-31)

5. the Eleven and other disciples (Matthew 28:16-20; Luke 24:36-49; John 20:19-23; 21:1-14; Acts 1:3-9; 1 Corinthians 15:5-6)

6. Thomas (John 20:24-29)

7. James (1 Corinthians 15:7)

8. Joseph and Matthias (Acts 1:22ff.)

9. 500 people at once (1 Corinthians 15:6)

10. Peter and John together (John 21:15-24)

11. Nathanael and some other disciples on the lake (John 21:1-14)

12. Paul (Acts 9:4ff.; 1 Corinthians 9:1; 15:8)

The mere fact that Jesus appears in different places to different people does not constitute a contradiction, as some critics allege. On any given day, each of us may appear in different places to different people. Given that there were at least 12 resurrection appearances, it is not surprising to find that among four independent writers some select certain details that the others do not.

Two important points are worth noting in this regard. First, all four accounts agree that the resurrection indeed happened. Second, these accounts give every evidence of frank and honest reporting. There is no cover-up. Even the disciples' doubts and skepticism are laid bare in the record. If the disciples had wanted to make up stories, would they not have left out these unflattering remarks about themselves?

Moreover, the different places where the accounts say Jesus appeared can be sensibly harmonized and thus freed from charges of contradiction and error.

> The chief difficulty relative to the recorded appearances
> is the place or places where they occurred. According to
> Saint Matthew our Lord appeared to the holy women

at Jerusalem, and to the disciples in Galilee at the mountain which He had appointed them....

Mark mentions no appearances at all, but in the appendix there is mention of several appearances which, however, are not localized.

Saint Luke's recorded appearances all took place in or near Jerusalem, while Saint John tells us of appearances which occurred both at Jerusalem and in Galilee.

Another difficulty is the command of Christ, delivered to the Apostles through the holy women, to go to Galilee; that there He would see them. This seems to be inconsistent with the appearances which He granted them the very evening of His resurrection at Jerusalem and at Emmaus....

It is certainly true that Jesus appointed Galilee as a rendezvous for the disciples. His first intention may probably have been to have the Apostles leave the hostile atmosphere of Jerusalem for the much more tranquil territory of Galilee, where He would show Himself to them and give them His final commission.

But the holy women delayed to report the direction to the Apostles, and when finally the message did reach them, they remained incredulous, labeled the report contemptuously "idle tales." The...most effective way to overcome this incredulity was for Jesus to appear to the Apostles directly, establish faith in their minds as to the reality of His resurrection and prepare them for the final and more important appearances in Galilee. I say more important because it was during these that Jesus imparted the great commission.[2]

Each Gospel writer's method and purpose account for the material included or omitted:

Matthew's method "is to pass over facts not pertinent to his plan, and to group in a synthetic picture the

facts he considers indispensable to his purpose. Since
the Evangelist's purpose is not to recount the doings
of the Apostles during Easter week at Jerusalem, he is
content with presenting us the disciples back in
Galilee." Thus he omits the Jerusalem appearances
entirely but by no means denies that they occurred.

Saint Luke's plan both in the Gospel and in the
Acts, as is well known, is geographical. Accordingly he
conducts Jesus and the Apostles through Galilee to
Jerusalem. There he concludes the story of Jesus, and
there he leaves the Apostles, to present them to us
again in his second volume, the Acts....We understand perfectly well why, according to the geographical plan, he does not concern himself with the
Galilean appearances, but sums up and localizes at
Jerusalem all the post-resurrection utterances of Jesus
which the Gospel's plan and purpose require.

There is therefore no well-founded objection
against the historical accuracy and trustworthiness of
the Gospel accounts of the events connected with the
resurrection. There is a natural and satisfying explanation of each of the pretended inconsistencies in the
four-fold record—satisfying for anyone who is willing
to be satisfied and is not obstinately determined to
reject the historic reality of the resurrection of Jesus
out of blind devotion to a philosophic postulate.[3]

Alleged Conflicting Traditions

Some critics have asserted that the resurrection accounts
contain "clearly contradictory historical traditions—one
placing all post-Crucifixion appearances in the Jerusalem area,
the other placing them in the region of Galilee."[4]

Hugh Schonfield, author of *The Passover Plot,* holds this
view of rival traditions:

> According to Luke…the "appearance" to the apostles
> is in the Judean tradition…This is at variance with
> the Galilean tradition followed by Matthew…In the
> Judean tradition Jesus positively identifies himself to
> the apostles in Jerusalem….We may regard the infor-
> mation as in the highest degree questionable in view of
> the rival record in Matthew, which suggests that the
> apostles did not see Jesus in Jerusalem.[5]

There are many possible reasons why Jesus would have
appeared to the disciples in Jerusalem and at other times in
Galilee. First, perhaps He simply had a lot to tell them, as the
Scriptures imply (John 16:12; Luke 24:27,45). Second, they
may have needed the time between appearances to absorb and
think through what Jesus was telling them. Third, He may
have wanted to appear in other locations to other disciples
who were absent at the times He appeared in areas closer to
Jerusalem.

The resurrection narratives tell us of 11 disciples and a
large number of other followers of Jesus who lived in towns
and places throughout Palestine. Obviously not every disciple
was in Jerusalem when Jesus first appeared there. It seems He
appeared to some disciples first in order to instruct them to
inform others of the time and place He would appear next.
That is perhaps one reason why the disciples went from
Jerusalem to Galilee—not only to meet Him there, but to tell
others not acquainted with the news that He would be there.

The Gospel evidence, therefore, does not support the
theory of rival traditions (for example, between Matthew and
Luke) limiting Jesus' resurrection appearances to either Galilee
or Jerusalem.

John and Luke both emphasize that there were many separate appearances of Jesus to His disciples. (To expect Jesus
would have appeared in only the same location over this

extended period of time does not make sense.) John, for example, in describing one of Jesus' appearances, specifies that "this was now the *third* time Jesus appeared to his disciples after he was raised from the dead" (21:14).

Matthew, moreover, reports not only a Galilean appearance (28:16), but a Jerusalem one as well (verse 9). John records both Jerusalem and Galilee appearances (chapters 20–21). Luke obviously recounts Jerusalem appearances, but in his second book, Acts, he also makes provision for Jesus' other appearances in different places: "After his suffering, he showed himself to these men and gave many convincing proofs that he was alive. He appeared to them over a period of forty days and spoke about the kingdom of God" (1:3; see also 10:40-41; 13:31).

And Mark records the message of the angels, "Go, tell his disciples and Peter, 'He is going ahead of you into Galilee. There you will see him'" (16:7). In brief, the evidence refutes the notion of rival traditions.

Can Other Discrepancies Concerning Jesus' Resurrection Appearances Be Resolved?

Our method for attempting to resolve the various alleged contradictions among the four Gospels has been to reconstruct plausible and logical sequences of events that explain the evidence and show that the accounts do not contradict. The discrepancies concerning Jesus' resurrection appearances in general are themselves easily answered in this way. Commentator Norval Geldenhuys offers one of many such cogent reconstructions:

> Very early on the Sunday morning the resurrection took place, the earthquake followed, the angel descended

and rolled away the stone (Matthew 28:2-4), and the guards of soldiers fled (Matthew 28:11).

A little later Mary Magdalene, Mary the mother of James and Salome hastened to the sepulcher while another group of women followed with the spices. Mary Magdalene reaches the sepulcher first, sees that it is empty and immediately goes to inform Peter and John (John 20:1ff.).

The other Mary and Salome approach and see the angel (Matthew 28:5). Thereafter the other women with Joanna among them come along; they see the two angels and receive the message that Jesus has risen (Luke 24:1ff.).

In the meantime Mary Magdalene reaches Peter and John, and they hasten to the sepulcher (John 20). Mary also follows them again and arrives at the sepulcher after the others have already departed.

She weeps at the sepulcher (John 20:2ff.) and sees the two angels, who ask her why she is weeping. After this she sees Jesus himself (John 20:14).

In the meantime the other women had gone to the other disciples and told them their experiences. But their words were regarded as idle tales (Luke 24:11) until Peter and John confirm them.

When the women were afterwards probably again on their way to the sepulcher, Jesus meets them (according to the true text of Matthew 28:9, which simply reads: "And behold, Jesus met them and said…").

Later in the day the Savior appeared to Peter alone (Luke 24:34; 1 Corinthians 15:5), toward evening to the men of Emmaus, and a little later to the whole group of disciples, with the exception of Thomas (Luke 24:36-43; John 20:19-24).

A week later he again appeared to the disciples, including Thomas, who was convinced of the certainty of the resurrection (John 21:1-23).

And during the forty days before his ascension the Lord also appeared in Galilee to the seven disciples at the Sea (John 21:1-23) (obviously the Galilean disciples, especially after Jesus' command that they should go thither, left Jerusalem after a few weeks for Galilee).

He also appeared to the five hundred of his followers in Galilee (as a result of the command of Mark 16:7 they would probably, after the reports concerning Jesus' resurrection had been brought to them, have assembled spontaneously in expectation of his appearance). When Paul wrote 1 Corinthians 15:6, most of the five hundred were still alive as living witnesses of the fact of the resurrection.

From Acts 1:3-4, and from the whole history from the commencement of Christianity, it appears that during the forty days before his ascension Jesus often appeared to his followers and spoke to them about many things in order to prepare them as builders of his church.

Toward the end of the forty days he no doubt commanded them to go to Jerusalem and to remain there until the promise of the Holy Ghost should be fulfilled.

After their return to Judaea the Savior also appeared to James (1 Corinthians 15:7) and to the apostles (Luke 24:33-53; Acts 1:3-12); and after his ascension he appeared to Paul near Damascus (Acts 9:3-6; 1 Corinthians 15:8) and again in the temple (Acts 22:17-21; 23:11).

Also Stephen, the first martyr, saw Jesus after his resurrection (Acts 7:55). Last of all, the Savior also appeared to John, the gray-haired exile on Patmos (Rev. 1:10-19).[6]

Although most of the apparent problems can be resolved by supplying a chronological sequence of events, it is not always possible to do so in every instance simply because we do not have sufficient information. The Gospels are primarily accounts of the apostles' preaching about Jesus. They are not complete biographies. Thus they do not supply us with an exact, detailed, and chronologically connected narrative of all the events they depict, as Geldenhuys explains:

> When we are faced with assertions (sometimes of a very arbitrary character) that the Gospels contradict one another as regards the particulars of the resurrection-appearances, we should bear in mind that the Gospels give such a condensed and selective account of the resurrection that no one knows whether the episodes described in one Gospel are the same as those mentioned in one or more of the others....And because we know so little of the less important particulars of those events, we are unable to see how the various narratives fit into one another. In any case, all the Gospels proclaim the main facts and leave no doubt as to the certainty that Jesus did arise.[7]

With the many details Matthew, Mark, Luke, and John report about Jesus' crucifixion, death, burial, and resurrection, hundreds of opportunities for the writers to contradict each other theoretically present themselves. After all, every single event, however small, mentioned by one writer, affords another writer the chance to contradict it.

But in all the details of the four resurrection narratives, we have found no proven contradiction and only a limited number of alleged contradictions—all of which have perfectly reasonable solutions on other grounds.* The fact of the resurrection, therefore, cannot be denied on the grounds that the accounts conflict.

---

* For additional study, see William Arndt, *Does the Bible Contradict Itself?* (St Louis, MO: Concordia, 1955); John W. Haley, *Alleged Discrepancies of the Bible* (New Kensington, PA: Whitaker House, 1996); Norman Geisler and Thomas Howe, *When Critics Ask: A Popular Handbook on Bible Difficulties* (Grand Rapids, MI: Baker, 1992); Gleason L. Archer, *Encyclopedia of Bible Difficulties* (Grand Rapids, MI: Zondervan, 1982).

THE MOST STUNNING
FACT OF FOREVER

SOON AFTER I BECAME A CHRISTIAN on April 23, 1971, I (John Weldon) read a short paper on the physical and medical aspects of a Roman crucifixion by a medical doctor. It had quite an impact, irrefutably demonstrating the immeasurable love God had for me. That He would actually endure such extreme physical torture for sinners and enemies was unthinkable.

For days I was struck by a simple fact. The unbearable torture of the crucifixion was almost infinitely less—nearly "nothing"—compared to the spiritual agony and torture Jesus must have endured when He bore the full weight of God's infinite wrath against all human sin, once for all.

That realization personally unchained God's love for me in a far more dramatic manner—indeed, to the point of making, in Chesterton's words, "dust and nonsense" of every other religion—simply because nothing in past or future history could ever conceivably approach it. In what other religion has it ever been heard, "God *so* loved the world..."?

After the Passion, the Empty Tomb

What could be more remarkable than the infinite God becoming man, dying on a cross, and then rising from the dead as proof of His offer to man of a free gift of eternal life?

Nothing—in all endless time.

Those who don't believe it rarely consider it, and they miss out on the most stunning fact of forever. But even for those of us who do believe, sometimes it's easy to become so familiar with the resurrection that we forget its immensity. It really is the final guarantee of eternal life. And without it, every one of the 1,200 promises in the Bible becomes meaningless.

> *No credible alternatives explain Jesus' personal nature other than what the Christian church has maintained for the past 2,000 years—that He is Lord and God.*

The resurrection makes the difference between meaning and despair, life and death, and everything in between, just as it did for me.

Just as in Jesus' day, some people today "say there is no resurrection"; some are open-minded, some closed; some oppose Christ's resurrection, some praise it (Matthew 22:23; Acts 4:2; 17:32). But no one can logically say it never happened.

In this book we have examined a fair portion of the evidence, which consistently supports the case for Jesus' resurrection. We have seen that

1. On numerous occasions Jesus foretold He would rise from the dead.

2. No credible alternatives explain Jesus' personal nature other than what the Christian church has maintained for the past 2,000 years—that He is Lord and God.

3. The facts of Jesus' death, the public location of the grave, the placing of the Roman guard and seal, and the empty tomb combine to form persuasive evidence for Jesus' resurrection.

4. The eyewitness testimony to the resurrection is unassailable given that it passed the strictest codes of what was considered valid, acceptable, legal testimony according to Jewish law—and that it could not be overturned despite the heavy opposition to, persecution of, and in many cases, eventual martyrdom of the eyewitnesses themselves.

5. The early and uncontested nature of the evidence as cited by Paul, especially that most of a group of 500 eyewitnesses who saw the resurrected Jesus were still living and thus were presumably available to affirm it (see 1 Corinthians 15:6), is dynamic proof of the resurrection.

6. Both the nature (physical and empirical) and extent (variety and number) of Jesus' resurrection appearances confirm He rose from the dead.

7. The disciples' great skepticism about the reports that Jesus had risen would have prevented their belief in the resurrection unless the evidence for it was compelling and beyond question (especially in the cases of Jesus' own brother, James, and doubting Thomas).

8. The very existence of the Christian church, including its day of rest and sacraments, is inexplicable apart from the resurrection. Their origin can be accounted for in no other manner.

9. The compatible yet independent nature of the four Gospel resurrection accounts strongly endorses their reliability—they do not contradict each other or show collusion.

10. The millions upon millions of changed lives of Christian converts throughout history, every one of them

claiming personal knowledge of the risen Christ, testify to the truth of the resurrection.

11. The continuing conversion of skeptics—many of whom originally set out to disprove the resurrection—indicates the strength of the evidence for it.

12. The resurrection is proven true by the powerful legal testimony in its behalf.

13. If Jesus had not risen from the dead, the New Testament could never have been written. The resurrection is absolutely central to all New Testament preaching, theology, and mission.

14. The complete lack of early published reports from hostile witnesses illustrates the strength of the evidence for the resurrection.

Of all the religions of the world, only Christianity provides an objective, verifiable test for its claims. That test is that Jesus rose bodily from the dead. Because of this, He has so impacted the world that no one today can consider themselves a truly educated person unless they know who He is. Moreover, since the resurrection can be substantiated as a fact of history, it verifies Christianity's claim to reveal absolute truths: truths concerning who God is, our purpose in life, what God requires of us, and what happens to us after we die. As with Jesus' followers, who at first struggled to believe the tomb was indeed empty, the resurrection demands from all people a response to the resurrected Christ and what He has done.

What Will You Do?

What do you intend to do with what you have learned in this book? For those of you who already know Christ as Savior, the overwhelming strength of the biblical testimony concerning Jesus' resurrection should strengthen your assurance that, as

God was at work redeeming the world through Jesus, His Son, He also continually wants to be at work in you, making you more like His Son.

For those of you who have not yet believed, we have seen that the resurrection evidence signifies the truthfulness of *all* of Jesus' claims. His resurrection affirms He is who He claimed to be—God incarnate, that is, God come down to us in bodily form.* It then is your duty to make a decision. Your eternal destiny depends on whether you believe in Him as your personal Savior.†

The Bible teaches that "all have sinned and fall short of the glory of God" (Romans 3:23), and that "the wages of sin is death, but the gift of God is eternal life in Christ Jesus our Lord" (Romans 6:23). All of us have sinned and broken God's laws. We need His forgiveness in order to enter into a personal relationship with Him and inherit eternal life. The gift is free. Anyone who wishes can receive Christ as their personal Savior by praying a prayer like the following. The exact words are not important, but you may wish to use this as a guide:

> *Dear God, I now turn from my sins. I ask Jesus Christ to enter my life and be my Lord and Savior. I realize that this is a serious decision and commitment, and I do not enter into it lightly. I believe that on the cross Jesus Christ died for my sins, and that He rose from the dead. I now receive Him into my life as my Lord and Savior. Help me to live a life that is pleasing to You and to Him. Amen.*

---

* John 1:1; 5:16-18; 8:58-59; 10:30-31; 14:6-9.
† See, for example, Matthew 20:28; 25:46; 26:28; John 3:16-18,36; 5:24.

Receiving Christ as your Savior involves a serious commitment. If you have prayed the prayer above, we encourage you to write us at The John Ankerberg Show so we may assist you in growing as a Christian. Some basic guidelines are:

1. Begin to read a modern, easy-to-read translation of the Bible, such as the New International Version (NIV) or the 1995 revision of the New American Standard Bible (NASB). Start with the New Testament, Psalms, and Proverbs and then proceed through the other books.

2. Find a church where people honor the Bible as God's Word and Christ as Lord and Savior.

3. Tell someone of your decision to follow Christ.

4. Begin to grow in your new relationship with God by talking to Him daily in prayer.

APPENDIXES

❦

If it is preached that Christ has been raised from the dead, how can some of you say that there is no resurrection of the dead? If there is no resurrection of the dead, then not even Christ has been raised. And if Christ has not been raised, our preaching is useless and so is your faith. More than that, we are then found to be false witnesses about God, for we have testified about God that he raised Christ from the dead. But he did not raise him if in fact the dead are not raised. For if the dead are not raised, then Christ has not been raised either. And if Christ has not been raised, your faith is futile; you are still in your sins. Then those also who have fallen asleep in Christ are lost. If only for this life we have hope in Christ, we are to be pitied more than all men. But Christ has indeed been raised from the dead.

1 Corinthians 15:12-20

Appendix A

The Uniqueness of Christianity and Its Empty Tomb

❧

Among all religions in the world, Christianity is unique. It claims the most famous teachings in history—the teachings of Jesus of Nazareth. It claims the most famous person in history—the person of Jesus of Nazareth. It claims the most famous death in history: the death of Jesus of Nazareth. And it claims the only resurrection in history.

Jesus Christ is unique in His miraculous birth and His miraculous life. He is unique in the content of His teaching and preaching. He is unique in the personal power He displayed over men and nature. He is unique in the degree of His love and compassion. He is unique in His sacrificial atoning death, physical resurrection from the dead, His ascension, and His self-predicted second coming.

Nevertheless, it is a common belief today that Christianity is not unique, because all religions are basically the same and all religious paths finally lead to the same God. But this idea flies directly in the face of the well-established facts of comparative religion. First, all religions are not the same; in terms of teachings and worldviews, they are as varied and discrepant as a hundred different philosophies.

Second, in terms of its claims, Christianity stands out like a lighthouse on a lonely shore. The Christian faith and the resurrection of Jesus Christ are of a singular nature:

- "The Christian claim maintains that, in the case of one whose life and teaching, whose miracles and impact were unparalleled, even death proved unable to hold him. Such a claim has never been made with any shred of credibility for any other person on this earth."[1]

- "Christianity alone has dared to claim" the resurrection of its central figure.[2]

- "Here is a teacher of religion and he calmly professes to stake his entire claims upon his ability, after having been done to death, to rise again from the grave. We may safely assume that there never was, before or since, such a proposal made."[3]

- "No founder of any world religion known to men ever dared say a thing like that."[4]

- "There is no record or claim of Resurrection in the case of any historical founder of religion."[5]

In essence, other religions believe in the teachings and philosophies of revered but long-dead founders—they never believe in a literal, physical resurrection of a living Savior.

- Buddha claimed to be only a man. He is still in the grave.

- Muhammad claimed to be only a prophet. He is still in the grave.

- Confucius claimed to be only a man. He is still in the grave.

- Moses was only a man and a prophet. He is still in the grave.

- Zoroaster was only a prophet. He is still in the grave.

- And so on…

No resurrection has ever occurred in history among any Hindu, Buddhist, Muslim prophets or leaders, nor among any other prophets or leaders in any other world religions—Shinto, Jainism, Sikhism, Baha'i, and so on. *No other founder of a religion actually proved that his religious claims and teachings were true in the manner Jesus Christ did.*

The resurrection proves that Christianity alone offers the way to God, and further, proves that the sincere inquirer after truth need not become confused or lost amid the jumble of religious claims the world offers:

> What religion in the world apart from the Judaeo-Christian faith, is intellectually coherent, morally dynamic, and big enough to embrace culture and science, creation and redemption, life and death, the individual (whatever his colour or class) and the community as well, the present generation and the future of mankind?…Christians…are claiming that almighty God took our human nature on him; that in that human nature he died, that he rose victorious over death, and will never die again.…
>
> If Jesus did rise from the dead, then he is indeed the way to God. God has vindicated him and set him on high. In that case the exclusiveness of the Christian claim makes sense. It does not amalgamate with other faiths, because it is so very different. The risen Jesus is not just one of the many, he is unique. It is not that Christians are narrow-minded or uncharitable about other faiths. But if Jesus is indeed, as the resurrection asserts, God himself who has come to our rescue, then

to reject him, or even to neglect him, is sheer folly. That is why Jesus is not, never has been, and never can be, just one among the religious leaders of mankind. He is not even the best. He is the only.[6]

Christianity Crumbles Without the Resurrection

If Christianity is restrictive when it comes to revelation and the way of salvation, at least it compensates for this by generosity of evidence and singularity of nature. If its claims are unique, so is its evidence and the manner by which it may be proven true or false.

In no other religion in the world is one single event so completely tied to the truth or falsehood of that religion. In every religion but Christianity the teachings of the originator are central, but the founder or prophet himself is not. The originator can be removed and little or nothing is altered. In other words, he makes little or no difference to the continued success of his religion.

To disprove Christianity during the time period following Jesus' death would have been far easier than most people realize.

However, in Christianity, Christ and His resurrection are central. Remove these and nothing credible remains of Christian faith.

In addition, the truth-claims of almost every other religion rest upon grounds that cannot be objectively determined. For example, Muhammad claimed to be the last major prophet of Allah, but never gave any evidence to prove this. Hinduism claims the world is the *maya* (illusion) of Brahman, while Buddhism maintains that enlightenment can be achieved only by destroying one's personality. Such things are difficult to prove.

But Christianity is unique in teaching that the truth of its doctrines can be determined by whether or not the resurrection occurred. If Christ rose again, His teachings and the doctrines derived from them must be true. For example, Christianity is the only religion in history that has ever taught that personal salvation is by grace through faith alone.* This particular doctrine is wholly dependent on the fact that the resurrection did occur, however.

To *disprove* Christianity during the time period following Jesus' death would have been far easier than most people realize. For example, consider a man today who becomes a religious prophet. Say that Swami Parapahabanana, who preaches in Oregon, predicts he will rise from the dead—and not only this, but will rise from the dead on the third day. His controversial religious actions and teachings eventually cause state "persecution." He is captured and charged with capital crimes. After a public trial, the man is found guilty and executed by electrocution in front of eyewitnesses, with some of his own critics among them. Further, his burial in a well-known local cemetery is also seen by his hundreds of followers and other eyewitnesses. In addition, the State of Oregon actually places a contingent of the National Guard at the tomb to prevent anyone from stealing the body to "fulfill" the swami's prophecies of a resurrection.

Now, would it be difficult at all to determine whether or not this man was ever resurrected from the dead? Of course not! Particularly since he has only *three days* in which to accomplish the event—and both the state and his enemies are committed to making sure no one can get to the grave to steal his body.

---

* John 3:16; 5:24; 6:47; 10:27-30; see also Ephesians 2:8-9.

But the same situation existed for Jesus in Jerusalem. Jesus' enemies were the most anxious of all to prove the resurrection had not occurred, while His own disciples had deserted Him and concluded that He was not their Messiah. Had the resurrection of Christ not occurred, it would have been known to everyone. But as we have seen previously, not only could no one disprove the resurrection *at that time*, but also subsequent events prove that it did happen.

Unique Within Its Own Era

The resurrection of Christ is also unique when compared to more ancient religions of the general early Christian era. In fact, the very idea of bodily resurrection was scoffed at. For example, in Stoicism, one's personal identity continued only until death or, in some forms, "possibly to the end of time but not forever."[7] Death was a desirable end to the sufferings of life, and some Stoics went so far as to recommend suicide.[8] Stoicism was also fatalistic and pantheistic. At death there was simply a cyclic re-absorption into the world soul or "deity."

For another example, Epicureanism, a materialistic philosophy, "taught that all existence consisted of atoms which might temporarily be organized in a certain form but which could change their form later to become a different substance."[9] But when the body was dissolved by death, the person ceased to exist. The idea that the body was absorbed into other elements or organisms was a strong barrier to the idea of physical resurrection from the dead.

Thus it is not surprising that when the apostle Paul spoke of the resurrection of the dead at Athens, Greece, the Stoics and Epicureans openly ridiculed him (Acts 17:18-32). The idea of an actual historical person being physically resurrected from the dead "was about as far from the minds of the Greeks as any New Testament truth could possibly be."[10]

In Plato's *Phaedo* we can observe that bodily resurrection is also contrary to Platonic principles and that "the doctrine of immortality had reached its highest point in Plato, and all subsequent writers who deal with the future life followed in his footsteps."[11]

All the foregoing is reinforced by the uniqueness of the particulars of the resurrection. For example, in regard to the three-day interval prior to the resurrection in John 10:17, Bible scholar Merrill Tenney observes,

> There is no duplicate of this phenomenon in classic pagan literature, nor is there any comparable instance of its association with resurrection. Only in the Old and New Testaments is the third day consistently related to the concept of a return from death; it is original with biblical revelation. In contrast to other religious teachers, who would not have dared to assert that they would die, and rise on a given day, Jesus plainly declared his intentions and fulfilled them, to the astonishment of all his followers.[12]

The Christian idea of the resurrection certainly did not derive from its religious environment. "The teaching of the New Testament came to the Greco-Roman world with a message which had not previously been proclaimed in the temples of the gods or in the halls of the philosophers. What was its origin?"[13] The only answer is, the actual resurrection of Jesus Christ!

Christianity Is Unique in Its Impact

Christianity is also unique in its effect at the individual and social level. Many things in life can lead to or force a significant or even radical change in a person's life—marriage, divorce, inheriting money, joining a cult. But the change brought about through a person's decision to trust in Christ as his or her personal Savior is unique. People's lives may change in other ways, but never in the manner that a life is changed by faith in Christ.

- It is unique in the ongoing moral reform it brings about.
- It is unique in the changed perspective it brings about.
- It is unique in its persistence.
- It is unique in its impact upon a person spiritually.*

When we consider the manner of change produced by non-Christian religion, we can see that committed members of other faiths experience a change produced by a combination of inner need or drive and an outward conformity to a system of rules and ethics. This may be characterized as a kind of self-reform; it is not a supernatural change. It is a shift in behavior, a personal reworking of priorities, and so on—but not a divinely wrought, radical inner alteration that transforms a person forever. Faith in Christ through the regeneration of the Holy Spirit (John 3:6-8; 6:63; 7:38-39) leads to a radical inward change that has permanent effects and can only be described as "eternal transformation."

Further, when people are converted to almost any other religion besides Christianity, they rarely claim this was entirely a product of God's grace that has brought them into a loving, personal relationship with the God of the universe. They will never claim it assures them of forgiveness of sins. They will never claim it guarantees them eternal life or personal immortality.

---

* Compare the 18 subdivisions of the biblical doctrine of salvation with what is offered in any other religion in the world: namely, imputation, grace, propitiation/atonement, reconciliation, calling, regeneration, union with Christ, conversion/repentance, faith, justification, adoption, sanctification, perseverance, election, redemption, resurrection.[14]

A Hindu never claims to come into a *personal* relationship with Brahman, for Brahman is impersonal. A Buddhist never claims to know Buddha *personally*, because Buddha no longer exists. At best he claims merely to be enlightened with the impersonal "Buddha nature." A Muslim does not claim to have come into an eternal, loving, *personal* relationship with either Muhammad or Allah. The prophet is still in the grave. A Muslim claims only that knowledge of the prophet's writings in the Qur'an may enable them to enter heaven, should their obedience and other conditions warrant it.

But a Christian claims to have come into a *personal,* eternal relationship with Jesus Christ at the moment of faith— because Jesus is still alive and in fact is the very God who made the universe (John 1:1-3; 5:24; 6:47).

Indeed, the kind of change produced by any other religion would simply not have been capable of generating the needed dynamism to establish the Christian church, given the conditions faced by the apostles both after the crucifixion (their dejection and depression) and in the early years of apostolic preaching (the severe persecution, and so on). As we have so clearly seen previously in this book, we simply cannot explain the changed lives of the apostles and the founding, spread, and continuance of the church based on any supposition other than that of the resurrection.

No Comparable Force for Good

Worldwide, the message of the resurrection has had a force for good that no other belief in the world has ever had. Nations and cultures have been altered. Bedrock changes have been made in people's view of themselves, God, society, and others. For 2,000 years, millions of families have been reunited after estrangement, immoral people have become godly, proud people humble, selfish individuals selfless and filled with love for other people. Incredible sacrifices have been made by Christians everywhere, the nature of which is impossible to explain unless the resurrection really occurred. One only need read the biographies of such believers as Hudson Taylor, Augustine, and countless others to see the kinds of changes Christ can bring to a life.

Further, we need only compare the practical results of the Judeo–Christian faith worldwide to that of any other faith to note the radical difference—and this difference can only be explained by the person and resurrection of Jesus Christ. As the noted historian Kenneth Scott Latourette observes:

> Through him movements have been set in motion which have made in society for what mankind believes to be its best—in the inward transformation of human lives, in political order, in the production and distribution of goods to meet the physical needs of men, in healing physical ills, in the relations between races and between nations, in art, in religion and in the achievement of the human intellect.
>
> Gauged by the consequences which have followed, the birth, life, death, and resurrection of Jesus have been the most important events in the history of man. Measured by his influence, Jesus is central in the human story.[15]

People become dissatisfied with movements and causes. But no one ever becomes dissatisfied with Jesus Christ. Endless millions of men and women have converted to Christianity from other isms, ideologies, and religions; hardly any have converted from genuine Christianity to any other system.

Why? Because Christianity has everything. Besides offering a personal relationship with God, the forgiveness of sins, and eternal life (not a bad start), it satisfies every aspect of the heart and mind of man. Its moral teachings and inducements to social good are unsurpassed. Christian philosophy and theology are unequalled in their profundity and cogency.

In fact, only by starting with the Christian beginning—the existence of an infinite, personal, triune God—do we have satisfying explanations for the deep philosophical questions men have asked in the area of metaphysics, ontology, epistemology, and morals. No other philosophy explains so much of the universe while simultaneously offering so much. Without it, modern Western science would probably never have existed. Without it there would be no U.S. Constitution, indeed, no America.[16]

Because of Christianity, the world's art, poetry, and music are richer. As the book *The World's Great Religions* observes of Jesus, "His life has inspired some of man's greatest creations—masterworks of poetry and music, of architecture, paintings and sculpture."[17]

〜

Only Christ's resurrection can adequately explain the tremendous impact He has had upon human history. Just as the Bible itself has had more impact on mankind than any other book (what other book in all of human history has ever caused the writing of so many other books, affected the destiny of so many lives—and even cultures—or been subjected to such intense critical scrutiny?), so Jesus Christ has had more impact than any other man. This is not merely the conclusion of Christian scholars, it is the general consensus of secular thought as well.

Christ changes people's lives because He is alive and has the power to do so. He is a living Savior, not a dead prophet. He is alive and powerful for every person who calls upon Him.

Appendix B

THEORIES THAT DENY
THE RESURRECTION

EVER SINCE THE TIME OF JESUS, critics have been attempting to re-explain His bodily resurrection naturalistically—uniformly assuming His body remained dead. Historically, many theories have been proposed, but not one of them "has ever met with general acceptance, even among radical critics and rationalists."[1] The following list is representative of the ideas that have surfaced over the years.[2]

The swoon theory claims that Jesus never died on the cross but merely "swooned." After His crucifixion (which included a spear thrust into the heart), He was taken down from the cross, wrapped in 75 pounds of linen and spices, and placed in a tomb. Yet somehow He revived. After three days without food or water, He unwrapped Himself (even though His arms had been pinned against His body and the spice-soaked linens had probably dried and hardened by this point), moved the one-to-two-ton stone from the grave entrance, and walked some distance on mutilated feet to find His disciples so He could falsely proclaim Himself to be the resurrected Messiah and conqueror of death. And the disciples believed Him! But if Jesus had not expired on the cross but only swooned, He still would have died sometime later—not exactly what one would expect of "the conqueror of death."

The "Passover Plot" theory. A version of the swoon theory, this notion asserts that Jesus plotted to fake His death to give the appearance He rose from the dead. He conspired with Judas to betray Him to the Jewish authorities and with Joseph of Arimathea to see to it that He was given a strong potion on the cross which would put Him into "a death-like trance." Appearing dead to the Roman authorities, He was to be taken off the cross and laid in a tomb—where He would revive after a short time and then reappear as "resurrected" to His disciples.

But the unexpected spear thrust led to His unforeseen death. Joseph had Him buried in an unknown tomb. The disciples, however, came upon the intended original place of burial, found the prearranged grave clothes, and falsely concluded from this that Jesus was alive.[3]

This theory makes Christ a fraud and the disciples near idiots. Moreover, if Christ was dead, how does one account for the many documented resurrection appearances?

The stolen or moved body theory proposes that the disciples stole or moved Jesus' body to make it appear He had been resurrected. This would make the disciples frauds. Moreover, this would have been unthinkable to them for several reasons: 1) They never *expected* Jesus to rise from the dead; 2) *all* of them would not have willingly remained silent about this lie in view of the likelihood that they would be killed for adhering to it; nor 3) would they have made God responsible for such a deception. Other versions of the theory propose that the Jews,

Romans, or Joseph of Arimathea moved the body, but for reasons no more compelling.

The hallucination/vision theory asserts that all people who had purportedly seen the resurrected Jesus—that is, the 12 disciples, the women, James (Jesus' brother), the crowd of 500 people—were eccentric visionaries or mentally ill. They hallucinated the risen Jesus through neurotic or psychotic visions. Unfortunately for this theory, all of the known characteristics of hallucination are entirely absent from the Gospel accounts of the encounters of Jesus' followers with their risen Lord.

More generally, the vision theory claims that the resurrected Jesus appeared to His followers through visions in the mind. This theory also does not fit the accounts. For example, what of doubting Thomas, who needed physical confirmation, and the crowd of 500, who simultaneously saw the risen Christ? What of Jesus Himself, who actively encouraged the disciples to touch Him physically to prove to them His resurrection (Luke 24:39; John 21)?

The telegram/telegraph theory suggests that the spiritually ascended Jesus telegraphed images of Himself from heaven to the minds of His followers on earth. These images were so graphic that they all mistakenly thought they had physically seen the resurrected Jesus in their midst. But what about the empty tomb? (The telegram theory also asserts that Jesus' body remained in the tomb.)

The mistaken-identity theory states that the 11 disciples, who had all but lived with Jesus for three years and never expected Him to rise from the dead, sometime after Jesus' death came to the conclusion He would come back to life. They then misidentified a complete stranger as the risen Jesus. Surely, though, they would have quickly recognized their error when conversing with the stranger or at least upon seeing him close up.

The wrong-tomb/grave-was-not-visited theory proposes that, although Jesus' followers saw where His body was buried, three days later they could not locate the tomb. They went to the wrong grave, which was empty, and incorrectly assumed from this that Jesus had been resurrected. There were, however, no resurrection appearances. The disciples concluded that Jesus had risen solely on the basis of an empty tomb—a tomb they were not certain was the correct one in the first place! This theory, however, places an exceedingly low intelligence quotient on the disciples, one greatly at odds with how the four Gospels present them.

The séance theory asserts that Jesus was "raised" in the same manner that a spirit is "raised" in a séance—through "ectoplasmic" manifestation. This is despite the fact that the theory makes Jesus' followers to be participants in a séance, a practice their own Scriptures sternly prohibited (see, for example, Deuteronomy 18:9-12). It also makes them out to be either liars or deluded for believing that something as ephemeral as an ectoplasmic manifestation was the same thing as a literal, physical resurrection appearance.

The annihilation theory claims that Jesus' body inexplicably disintegrated into nothingness. It has received no support.

The "Jesus never existed" and resurrection-as-legend theories. The first of these proposes that Jesus was a fraudulent invention of the disciples, a legend. It too has no support. But the second, a variation of the first, has held more sway. It asserts that the followers of Jesus derived the resurrection story from similar stories of contemporary Greco–Roman mystery cults. It sees Jesus as a historical person, but considers the resurrection as strictly legendary. The dissimilarity, however, between the mystery cults of the first century and early Christianity is far too great; moreover, the early church consistently opposed such assimilation.*

The Failure of the Theories

Anyone who takes the time to compare these theories to the four Gospel resurrection accounts quickly discovers that they are highly inferior explanations, grossly conflicting at many points with each other and more importantly with the biblical evidence itself. No one yet has proposed a theory that *reasonably* accounts for all the historical data to the satisfaction of believer and skeptic alike. In fact, as author and researcher Gary Habermas observes,

> One interesting illustration of this failure of the naturalistic theories is that they were disproven by the nineteenth-century older liberals themselves, [the very ones] by whom these theories were popularized. These scholars refuted each other's theories, leaving no viable naturalistic hypotheses....Twentieth-century critical scholars have generally rejected naturalistic theories as a whole, judging that they are incapable of explaining the known data....That even such critical scholars have rejected these naturalistic theories is a significant epitaph for the failure of these views.[4]

Since the time of Christ, no attempt to offer conclusive proof against the bodily resurrection has succeeded. This in itself is significant. Every alternate theory is more difficult to believe than the belief that Jesus physically rose from the dead, a conviction shared by all four Gospel writers and all New Testament teaching on this point. And as we have seen

---

* See appendix C for more about the mystery religions.

in the preceding chapters, this conviction is most compelling. Here is a chart that briefly notes the evidence against the alternate theories:

DISPROOF OF RATIONALISTIC THEORIES TO EXPLAIN THE EMPTY TOMB

Alternate Theory	Disproof of Theory
Swoon theory	Jesus' death and burial; Paul's conversion
"Passover Plot" theory	Messianic prophecy that would have been impossible for Jesus to fulfill; resurrection appearances
The stolen body theory	The facts of human psychology, the disciples' conviction concerning the resurrection; their uniform testimony and martyrdom
The hallucination theory	The disciples' mental state and experiences of Jesus; the nature of Jesus' appearances versus the nature of hallucinations
The telegram/telegraph/telepathic theory	The nature of Jesus' appearances to the disciples (physical, external, running conversations, and so on); these are indistinguishable from a literal physical resurrection
Mistaken-identity theory	The disciples spent three years with Jesus and knew Him intimately
The wrong-tomb theory	The fact of the publicly known burial site; eyewitness accounts of the burial
The séance theory	The law and tradition of Jesus' followers and their observational ability
The annihilation theory (the body just evaporated)	The resurrection appearances, the existence of the church
Jesus was a legend, an invention	The resurrection appearances, human psychology, the history of skeptics' conversion
Derived from the mystery religions	Too great a dissimilarity; the historical improbability of any influence of the mystery cults in Palestine in the third and fourth decade of the first century; the consistent opposition to such mystery cults by the early church

Theologically, the severest criticism of these theories is that they make God responsible for a lie. The undisputed teaching of the Gospel accounts and of the rest of the New Testament is that God raised Jesus bodily from the dead. But according to these theories, Jesus' body never left the tomb. For the 11 disciples, all of whom were Jewish, to make God responsible for a work He *clearly* did not do would have been unthinkable.

In the end, facts will always win because facts, unlike mere opinion, cannot be changed or disproven. The twentieth- and twenty-first-century theories proposed to explain away the resurrection are no better, and they suffer the same fate as their nineteenth-century counterparts.

Appendix C

THE RESURRECTION OF CHRIST AND THE MYSTERY RELIGIONS

⚬≫⚬

DESPITE THEIR GREAT AGE, the ancient mystery religions sport a considerable influence even today. One prominent example is the neo-Gnostic bestselling murder mystery by Dan Brown, *The DaVinci Code* (2003). In its first year alone the book sold more than five million copies, and at least a dozen additional books have been written about it. However, its attempt to discredit historic Christianity and acclaim the sacred feminine is replete with historical and theological errors, one of which correlates Christianity and the ancient mystery religions, specifically Mithraism.[1]

But this is nothing new. Seemingly offering more credibility, many university and college courses in Christianity or comparative religion have also expressed the view that Christianity is merely a variation of this more ancient religious theme. They teach that Christian faith developed from or was influenced by the ancient pagan mystery religions of Rome, Greece, Egypt, and other areas. The conclusion is that the Christian faith is not unique (as it claims), but is at best an imitation faith, hoping to be something it is not. Numerous "parallels" are drawn between the motif in these religions of "dying and rising savior–gods," and the centrality of the death and resurrection of Jesus Christ in the Christian faith. From this it is asserted that certainly, or at least probably, Christianity was merely a later, revisionist form of such pagan religion.

In the last hundred years, numerous books have been written which attempt to defend this idea.* More recently, this concept has been popularized by the late mythologist Joseph Campbell in *The Power of Myth, The Masks of God,* and other books, also largely as a means to "discredit" Christianity.

> One assumption inherent in interpreting Christianity as an embellished mystery religion is that the Christian faith per se is the invention of men, not a revelation from God.

What were the mystery religions? Allegedly, their teachings were revealed by the Egyptian god Thoth. They were eclectic religious cults that stressed nature religion, oaths of secrecy, brotherhood, and spiritual quest. They offered rites of initiation that were associated with or dedicated to various gods and goddesses of the ancient world. In fact, these rites often inculcated contact, or "union," with the "gods" (spirits). Participants hoped to attain knowledge, power, and immortality from their worship and contact with these gods. In essence, the mystery religions were part and parcel of the world of the occult in ancient Europe and Asia. They were idolatrous, opposed Christian teachings, and not infrequently engaged in barbarous or immoral practices.[2]

Nevertheless, it was the theme of alleged dying and rising savior–gods that initially sparked the interest of some scholars

---

* Among these are J.M. Robertson's *Pagan Christs* (New Hyde Park, NY: University Books, 1967) and Kersey Graves' *The World's Sixteen Crucified Saviors or Christianity Before Christ* (New Hyde Park, NY: University Books, 1971). This idea has also formed one line of argumentation for the larger theme that Jesus never even existed, as in G.A. Wells' *Did Jesus Exist?* (Buffalo, NY: Prometheus Books, 1975).

and many skeptics as to whether or not Christianity was a derivative of the mysteries. For example, if there had been religious cults in Palestine at the time of Christ that believed in a mythological central figure who periodically died and came back to life in harmony with certain agricultural–fertility cycles, it could be argued that Christianity was merely the offshoot of these beliefs and that its distinctive theological teachings were later inventions.

If true, Christianity would have been only a variation of an earlier pagan religious worldview, a religion that later evolved its distinctive theological doctrines—for example, Christ's being the unique incarnation of God and Savior of man. In fact, in this scenario, the biblical Jesus need never even have existed. After all, the mysteries were based on mythical gods. Hence, some critics (not, in general, historians) argue that Jesus was only an invented figure patterned after the life cycles of mythological gods such as Attis, Cybele, Osiris, Mithra, Adonis, Demeter, Persephone, Dionysus, and others.

One assumption inherent in interpreting Christianity as an embellished mystery religion is that the Christian faith per se is the invention of men, not a revelation from God. As a result, virtually all the unique teachings of New Testament theology, are viewed as mere religious innovation after the fact. For example, concerning Jesus Christ this would mean His incarnation and virgin birth, miracles and teachings, atonement for sin, physical resurrection from the dead, promised return, and so on, are not historical facts, but later revisions of pagan stories. The cardinal teachings of orthodox Christianity become lies and falsehoods, a conclusion that warms the heart of some people today.

Uncovering the Actual Mythologies

Unfortunately for skeptics, when theories involving the mystery traditions are objectively examined and compared with Christianity, only superficial similarities remain—because Christianity and the mystery religions are as distinct as night and day.[3] Even secular scholars have rejected the idea that Christianity borrowed from the ancient mysteries. For instance, the well-respected Sir Edward Evans-Pritchard writes in *Theories of Primitive Religion* that "the evidence for this theory...is negligible."[4]

In fact, the gods of the mysteries are not even resurrected; at best they are only resuscitated within the context of a gross mythology:

- Samuel N. Kramer's thorough work showed that the alleged resurrection of Tammuz (a fertility god of Mesopotamia) was based on "nothing but inference and surmise, guess and conjecture."[5]

- Pierre Lambrechts maintains that in the case of the alleged resurrection of Adonis no evidence exists, either in the early texts or the pictorial representations. The texts which refer to a resurrection are quite late, dating from the second to the fourth centuries AD.[6]

- Lambrechts also reveals that for Attis there is no suggestion he was a resurrected god until after AD 150.[7]

- In the case of Adonis, there is a lapse of at least 700 years.[8]

- The cult of Isis and Osiris ends with Osiris becoming lord of the underworld while Isis regathers his dismembered body from the Nile River and subsequently magically restores it. E.A. Wallace Budge, an authority on ancient religions, declares that "there is nothing in the texts which justify the assumption that Osiris knew he would rise from the dead, and that he would become king and judge of the dead, or that Egyptians believed that Osiris died on their behalf and rose again in order that they might also rise from the dead."[9]

To sum up this point, "the idea that the god dies and rises again to lead his worshippers to eternal life does not exist in any Hellenic mystery religion."[10] It would appear then, that the real mythology is in the minds of skeptics who are confusing mystery-religion beliefs with the historical person and work of Jesus of Nazareth. Indeed, noted scholars long ago refuted the idea that Christianity is related to the mysteries.

For instance, former atheist and Cambridge and Oxford scholar C.S. Lewis emphasized that, in contrast to the gods of the mysteries,

> Jahweh is clearly *not* a Nature-God. He does not die and come to life each year as a true corn-king should....He is not the soul of Nature nor any part of Nature. He inhabits eternity; he dwells in the high and holy place; heaven is his throne, not his vehicle; earth is his footstool, not his vesture. One day he will dismantle both and make a new heaven and earth. He is not to be identified even with the "divine spark" in man. He is "God and not man." His thoughts are not our thoughts.[11]

In fact, Lewis had previously noted that upon his first serious reading of the New Testament, he was "chilled and puzzled by the almost total absence of such ideas in the Christian documents."[12] In other words, he was familiar with the theories suggesting resemblance between Christianity and the mysteries, expected to find them, and was shocked to discover their absence.

The great comparative religion scholar Mircea Eliade

> published in *Patterns of Initiation* a series of lectures he had given at the University of Chicago in the fall of

1956. In one of those lectures, Eliade said recent research did not support the theories that the origin of Christianity was influenced by pagan mystery cults. "There is no reason to suppose that primitive Christianity was influenced by the Hellenistic mysteries," said Eliade. In fact, the reverse may actually be true:

> The renaissance of the mysteries in the first centuries of our era may well be related to the rise and spread of Christianity....Certain mysteries may well have reinterpreted their ancient rites in the light of the new religious values contributed by Christianity.

Eliade added that it was only much later, when Christianity had to compete with the renaissance of the mystery cults, that Christians began to borrow from the religious symbols of these cults. They did this in order to help them explain their religion to others (not to modify it), thereby hoping to win converts.[13]

Opposition, Not Derivation

There is simply no evidence that the mystery religions exerted any influence in Palestine in the first three decades of the first century. Where did the material supposedly originate to make Christianity a mystery religion? Why would such parallels even be suggested?[14] The manuscripts we possess prove that the teachings of Jesus and Paul are the ones given in the New Testament; there was simply not sufficient time for the disciples to be influenced by the mysteries even if they were open to the idea, which they weren't.

Finally, when the influence of the mysteries did reach Palestine—principally through gnosticism—the early church did not accept it but renounced it vigorously as trafficking in pagan myths. The complete lack of syncretism is difficult to explain if Christianity was ultimately a derivative of such paganism.

Indeed, Christianity waged uncompromising intellectual and spiritual warfare against the mystery religions and their varied moral and theological deficiencies. We can give a snapshot of these deficiencies as follows:

> The initiation ceremonies usually mimed death and resurrection. This was done in the most extravagant manner. In some ceremonies, candidates were buried or shut up in a sarcophagus; they were even symbolically deprived of their entrails and mummified (an animal's belly with entrails was prepared for ceremony). Alternately, the candidates were symbolically drowned or decapitated. In imitation of the Orphic myth of Dionysus Zagreus, a rite was held in which the heart of a victim, supposedly a human child, was roasted and distributed among the participants to be eaten....In the Dionysus and Isis mysteries, the initiation was sometimes accomplished by a "sacred marriage," a sacral copulation.[15]

Again, if Christianity were really simply a derivation of such mystery religions, why did it so staunchly oppose them? The only explanation is that no such similarity existed because Christianity always was what it always claimed—a unique revelation from God.

We may summarize by noting the research of philosopher of religion Dr. Ronald H. Nash. In *Christianity and the Hellenistic World*, he notes that despite the fact that many scholars still argue that early-first-century Christianity took some or many of its fundamental beliefs and practices from pagan religions, scholars in the disciplines of classical and biblical studies regard this claim as dubious at best.

Nash points out that the death of Jesus is distinct from the deaths of the pagan gods in at least half a dozen different ways.[16] For example:

- None of the dying and rising "savior–gods" ever died for someone else, and they never claimed to die for sin. The concept of the incarnate Son of God undergoing a propitiatory, substitutionary death for man is a doctrine wholly unique to Christianity.

- In addition, biblically, Jesus died one time for all sin, whereas the pagan gods were, for example, vegetation deities who mimicked the annual cycles of nature in their repeated deaths and resuscitations.

- Further, Jesus died in space–time history, whereas the pagan deities were simply myths. They could hardly die when they never had life to begin with.

- Finally, Jesus died voluntarily, and His death was a victory, not a defeat, both of which factors stand in contrast to concepts found in the pagan cults.

Regardless of the major biblical doctrine we are referring to, whether it be the nature of God, the incarnation, redemption, the resurrection, or the new birth, none of these reveals any dependence whatsoever upon the mystery religions.

"The tide of scholarly opinion has turned dramatically against attempts to make early Christianity dependent on the so-called dying and rising gods of Hellenistic paganism,"[17] concludes Nash. He summarizes eight of the most serious weaknesses in such theories as follows:[18]

1. Similarity does not prove dependence. The fact that some similarities exist between Christianity and the mysteries no more prove Christianity was derived from them than similarities between dogs and cats prove dogs derived from cats.

2. Even the alleged similarities "are either greatly exaggerated or invented."

3. "The chronology is all wrong" because the basic beliefs of Christianity were in existence in the first century, while the full development of the mystery religions did not happen until the second century. And historically, it is unlikely that any significant encounter took place between Christianity and the pagan mystery religions until the third century.

4. As a devout Jew, the apostle Paul would never have considered borrowing his teachings from pagan religion. There is not the slightest hint of pagan beliefs in his writings.

5. As a monotheistic religion with a coherent body of doctrine, Christianity could hardly have borrowed from a polytheistic and doctrinally contradictory paganism.

6. First-century Christianity was an exclusivistic faith, not a syncretistic one—which it would have become had borrowing been significant.

7. Christianity is demonstrably grounded in the actual events of history, not myths.

8. If any borrowing did occur, it was undoubtedly the other way around. In other words, as Christianity grew in influence and expanded in the second and third centuries, the pagan systems, recognizing the threat, would be likely to borrow elements of Christianity to

capitalize upon its success. (For instance, the pagan rite of bathing in bull's blood—*taurobolium*—initially was said to hold its spiritual efficacy for 20 years. But the cult of Cybele, when it recognized that Christians were promised eternal life by faith in Jesus, raised the efficacy of their rite "from 20 years to eternity.")

The best way for anyone to refute the idea of any derivation of Christianity from the mystery cults is simply to study the mystery religions and compare them carefully with the teachings of the New Testament.

NOTES

❦

What Next?

1. David Sloan, "Two Zen Men and a Christian at *The Passion*," www.godspy .com/reviews/Two-Zen-Men-and-a-Christian-at-the-Passion.cfm.

Chapter 1—The First Act of an Eternal Drama

1. www.beliefnet.com/story/141/story_14185_1.html.

2. J. Lee Grady, "I Call This a Miracle," www.beliefnet.com/story/141/story_ 14107_1.html

3. *The Barna Update*, "New Survey Examines the Impact of Gibson's 'Passion'" Movie, July 10, 2004 (survey taken May 24-28, 2004), www.barna.org/Flex Page.aspx?Page=BarnaUpdateNarrow&BarnaUpdateID=167.

4. www.barna.org/FlexPage.aspx?Page=BarnaUpdate&BarnaUpdateID=167. Based on a 100-million viewing audience.

5. Opening February 27, 2004, in its first four months the film took in $370 million domestically, becoming number seven on the all-time U.S. domestic box-office chart (www.newsmax.com/archives/ic/2004/3/19/135600.shtml). Additional international sales, movie rentals, DVD, CD, music, and related sales, as well as current "passion tours" and ministry use for evangelism, not to mention eventual TV and Internet showings, could place the viewing audience at a billion within the next decade.

6. www.newsmax.com/archives/ic/2004/3/19/135600.shtml.

7. See www.christianitytoday.com/ct/2004/006/13.19.html. "This film is generating huge interest in Jesus and the Bible," according to missionaries. *AsiaNews* reported that "Middle East Christians are spellbound by the interest Arabs have taken in seeing the Gospel portrayed on the big screen... Many Arabs were interested in seeing the film only because of the anti-Semitic controversy surrounding it. However the movie's theme is

an unavoidable subject. 'The message of loving your enemies and Jesus who, even while up on the cross, prayed for and forgave them strikes all viewers deeply,' said two Americans working in Qatar" (www.asianews.it/view.php?l =en&art=600).

8. Unless otherwise indicated, all Scripture quotations in this chapter are taken from the NIV (New International Version).

9. Adapted from ThePassionofChrist.com.

10. C. Truman Davis, MD, "Medical Account of Crucifixion," Arizona Medical Association's *Arizona Medicine,* March 1965.

11. Davis.

12. Three religious, three civil: before Annas in his house, before Caiaphas at his palace, before Caiphas and the Sanhedrin, before Pilate, before Herod, and before Pilate again. See Clifford Wilson, *The False Trials of Jesus Christ* (Oklahoma City: Hearthstone Publishing, Ltd., 1994; or http://biblia.com/jesus bible/passion10.htm).

13. Davis.

14. William D. Edwards, MD; Wesley J. Gabel, and Floyd E. Hosmer, "On the Physical Death of Jesus Christ, *The Journal of the American Medical Association,* vol. 255, no. 11 (March 21, 1986).

15. David Terasaka, MD, "Medical Aspects of the Crucifixion of Jesus Christ," 1996, www.new-life.net/crucify1.htm.

16. Terasaka.

17. Davis.

18. Davis.

19. Joe E. Zias, "Crucifixion in Antiquity," www.apologeticspress.org/rr/rr2002/ r&r0201a.htm.

20. Richard P. Bucher, "Crucifixion in the Ancient World," http://users.rcn.com/ tlclcms/crucify.htm.

21. Edwards, et al.

22. Edwards, et al.

23. Terasaka.

24. Edwards, et al.

25. Edwards, et al.

26. Davis.

27. Davis

28. Edwards et al.

29. If Jesus carries the marks of His crucifixion on His resurrected body, it may explain *both* the inability and ability of some to recognize Him in His resurrection state: "In eternity, Jesus will bear the marks of His crucifixion.

Revelation 5:6 suggests that He appears in heaven with the marks as a Lamb *'looking as if it had been slain.'* We know that when He appeared to Thomas He bore the scars of the nails and the spear in His side (John 20:26-28). It is also worth considering reasons as to why He was not immediately recognized after His resurrection. In John 21:12, it is stated that the disciples did *'not dare to ask Him His identity, because they knew that it was the Lord.'* It is possible that His resurrection body still has the marks of His beatings. *'The body of His glorification will be the body of His humiliation'"* (Terasaka).

30. www.godspy.com/culture/The-Unbearable-Reality-of-Love-The-Passion-of -The-Christ.cfm

31. Luke 24:25-26,44-47; John 3:14-18; 8:23-28; 10:36-37; Acts 2:31-32; Romans 1:4; 14:9.

32. Matthew 20:28; 26:28; John 3:14; 5:24-29; 6:37-40; 10:27-30; 11:25; Acts 10:43; Romans 4:25.

33. Acts 17:31; John 5:24-25; 6:40; 8:24.

34. John 4:40-42; 10:7-9,17-18; 14:3,6; Acts 4:10-12; 1 Timothy 2:5.

Part I—Evidence for the Resurrection

1. Charles Guignebert, *Jesus* (New York: np, 1935), p. 536; as cited in Wilbur M. Smith, *The Supernaturalness of Christ* (Grand Rapids, MI: Baker, 1974), pp. 189-190.

2. David F. Strauss, *A New Life of Jesus,* vol. 1 (London, np, 1965), pp. 41,397; as cited in Smith, p. 190.

3. For a cogent philosophical defense of miracles, see C.S. Lewis, *Miracles* (London: Fontana, 1970); Colin Brown, *Miracles and the Critical Mind* (Grand Rapids, MI: Eerdmans, 1984).

Chapter 2—Jesus' Death and Burial—and the Empty Tomb

1. Bernard Ramm, *Protestant Christian Evidences* (Chicago: Moody, 1971), p. 186.

2. See, e.g., P. Barbet, MD, *A Doctor at Calvary* (Garden City, NJ: Doubleday, 1963); E.S. Thompson, MD, *On the Physical Cause of the Death of Christ* (London: SPCK, 1984); W.M. Edwards, MD et al., "A Medical Report: On the Physical Death of Jesus Christ," *PM* (April/May 1987).

3. Michael Green, *The Empty Cross of Jesus* (Downers Grove, IL: InterVarsity Press, 1984), p. 93.

4. Merrill Tenney, *The Reality of the Resurrection* (Chicago: Moody, 1972), p. 106.

5. For example., H.E.G. Paulus, *Das Leben Jesus* [English, *The Life of Jesus*] (1828).

6. Wilbur M. Smith, *Therefore Stand* (Grand Rapids, MI: Baker, 1972), p. 371.

7. John Wenham, *The Easter Enigma* (Grand Rapids, MI: Zondervan, 1984), p. 71.

8. Tenney, p. 110; Josh McDowell, *Evidence that Demands a Verdict*, vol. 1, 2nd ed. (San Bernardino, CA: Here's Life Publishers, 1979), p. 207.

9. McDowell, *Evidence*, p. 208.

10. Robertson, *Word Pictures*, vol. 1, p. 239; as cited in McDowell, *Evidence*, p. 209.

11. Dionysius of Halicarnassus, *Antiquities of Rome*, viii. 79, and Polybius, vi. 37-38; as cited in George Currie, *The Military Discipline of the Romans from the Founding of the City to the Close of the Republic* (1928); as cited in McDowell, *Evidence*, pp. 212-213.

12. See further Currie's documentation of this as cited in McDowell, *Evidence*, p. 213.

13. See T.G. Tucker, *Life in the Roman World of Nero and St. Paul* (New York: Macmillan, 1910), pp. 342-344; as cited in McDowell, *Evidence*, p. 214.

14. Smith, pp. 373-374.

15. Matthew 26:65-66; John 7:19,30; 8:40,59; 11:53,57.

16. As cited in Josh McDowell, *More Than a Carpenter* (Wheaton, IL: Tyndale, 1983), pp. 91-92.

17. J.N.D. Anderson, *Christianity: The Witness of History* (London: Tyndale, 1970), p. 96.

18. R.A. Torrey, "The Certainty and Importance of the Bodily Resurrection of Jesus Christ from the Dead," rev. and ed. G.B. Stanton, in *The Fundamentals for Today*, ed. C.L. Feinberg (Grand Rapids, MI: Kregel, 1964), p. 274.

19. Green, p. 98, emphasis in original.

20. Frank Morison, *Who Moved the Stone?* (Downers Grove, IL: InterVarsity Press, 1969), p. 94.

21. D.H. Van Daalen, as quoted in William Lane Craig, *The Son Rises* (Chicago: Moody, 1981), pp. 84-85, 88.

22. Norval Geldenhuys, *Commentary on the Gospel of Luke* (Grand Rapids, MI: Eerdmans, 1975), p. 629.

Chapter 3—Jesus' Resurrection Appearances

1. John R.W. Stott, *The Epistles of John*, The Tyndale New Testament Commentary (Grand Rapids, MI: Eerdmans, 1977), p. 60.

2. Josh McDowell, *More Than a Carpenter* (Wheaton, IL: Tyndale, 1983), p. 61.

3. Michael Green, *The Empty Cross of Jesus* (Downers Grove, IL: InterVarsity Press, 1984), p. 97.

4. William Lane Craig, *The Son Rises* (Chicago: Moody, 1981), p. 125; see also Wolfhart Pannenberg, *Jesus: God and Man*, tr. L.L. Wilkins and D.A. Priebe (London: SCM, 1968), pp. 88-99.

5. Green, p. 114.

6. Green, p. 115.

7. Craig, pp. 116-117.

8. Leland E. Hinsie, MD, and Robert Jean Campbell, MD, *Psychiatric Dictionary*, 4th ed. (New York: Oxford, 1970), pp. 333-336; Paul H. Hoch et al., eds., *Psychopathology of Perception* (New York: Grune and Stratton, 1965); see also Green, pp. 118-119; W.J. Sparrow-Simpson, *The Resurrection and Modern Thought* (London: Longmans, 1911), pp. 389-390.

9. This chart is taken from Norman L. Geisler, *The Battle for the Resurrection* (Nashville, TN: Thomas Nelson, 1984), p. 141; references are added.

10. Craig, p. 117.

11. Wilbur M. Smith, *The Supernaturalness of Christ* (Grand Rapids, MI: Baker, 1974), p. 199, emphasis in original.

12. Merrill Tenney, *The Reality of the Resurrection* (Chicago: Moody, 1972), pp. 123-124.

Chapter 4—The Powerful Evidence of Skepticism

1. Josh McDowell, *More Than a Carpenter* (Wheaton, IL: Tyndale, 1983), pp. 64-65.

2. On Jesus as the Messiah, see further John Ankerberg and John Weldon, *The Case for Jesus the Messiah* (Eugene, OR: Harvest House Publishers, 1989); John Ankerberg and John Weldon, *The Facts on Jesus the Messiah* (Eugene, OR: Harvest House Publishers, 1993).

3. Irwin H. Linton, *A Lawyer Examines the Bible: A Defense of the Christian Faith* (San Diego: Creation Life, 1977), p. 193.

4. William Lane Craig, *The Son Rises* (Chicago: Moody, 1981), pp. 128-130, emphasis in original.

5. Craig, p. 131.

6. Norval Geldenhuys, *Commentary on the Gospel of Luke* (Grand Rapids, MI: Eerdmans, 1975), p. 628.

7. Wilbur M. Smith, *Therefore Stand* (Grand Rapids, MI: Baker, 1972).

8. Smith, pp. 367-368.

9. Frank Morison, *Who Moved the Stone?* (Downers Grove, IL: InterVarsity Press, 1969), pp. 115-116, emphasis in original.

10. Merrill Tenney, *The Reality of the Resurrection* (Chicago: Moody, 1972), p. 140.

11. Michael Green, *The Empty Cross of Jesus* (Downers Grove, IL: InterVarsity Press, 1984), p. 95.

12. Geldenhuys, p. 629.

13. See, for example, John Warwick Montgomery, "How Muslims Do Apologetics," in *Faith Founded on Fact* (New York: Nelson, 1978); D. Johnson, *A Reasoned Look at Asian Religions* (Minneapolis: Bethany, 1985); S.C. Hackett, *Oriental Philosophy* (Madison: Univ. of Wisconsin, 1979); John Ankerberg and John Weldon, *The Facts on Islam* and *The Facts on Hinduism in America* (Eugene, OR: Harvest House Publishers, 1992); John Weldon, *Buddhism and Nichiren Shoshu Buddhism: A Critique* (MA thesis, Anaheim, CA: Simon Greenleaf University, 1987), pp. 86-99.

14. Henry Morris, *Many Infallible Proofs* (San Diego: Master Books, 1982), p. 1, emphasis in original.

15. John Warwick Montgomery, *Evidence for Faith* (Richardson, TX: Probe Books, 1991), p. 9.

16. T.C. Muck, "Truth's Intrepid Ambassador," *Christianity Today*, November 1990, p. 34.

17. *Chambers' Encyclopedia*, vol. 10 (London: Pergamon, 1966), p. 516; as cited in McDowell, *More Than a Carpenter*, p. 86.

18. A. Harnack, "Alexandria, School of," in *The New Schaff-Herzog Encyclopedia of Religious Knowledge*, vol. 1 (Grand Rapids, MI: Baker, 1977), pp. 124-125,347; L.R. Bush, ed., *Classical Readings and Christian Apologetics: A.D. 100-1800* (Grand Rapids, MI: Zondervan, 1983), p. 31.

19. Bush, pp. 195-198.

20. A copy of these letters can be found in most university libraries under *Early American Imprints* #8909 (1639–1800) of the American Antiquarian Society.

21. *Early American Imprints* #8909, p. 3.

22. Morison, pp. 9-11.

23. Josh McDowell, *Evidence that Demands a Verdict*, vol. 1, 1st ed. (San Bernardino, CA: Here's Life Publishers, 1979), p. 373.

24. Unpublished debate between John Warwick Montgomery and John K. Naland, televised April 1990 on *The John Ankerberg Show*.

25. John Warwick Montgomery, "Introduction to Apologetics," class notes, The Simon Greenleaf School of Law (Anaheim, CA: January, 1986).

26. C.S. Lewis, *Surprised by Joy* (New York: MacMillan, 1955), pp. 175, 191, 229, 228.

27. Lee Strobel, *The Case for Christ* (Grand Rapids, MI: Zondervan, 1998), pp. 15,16.

28. Strobel, pp. 356-359.

29. Strobel, pp. 361-365.

30. E.A. Rowell, *Prophecy Speaks* (Tacoma Park: Review and Herald, 1933), pp. 195-197, as cited in McDowell, *Evidence that Demands a Verdict*, p. 366.

31. William M. Ramsay, *The Bearing of Recent Discovery on the Trustworthiness of the New Testament* (Grand Rapids, MI: Baker, 1959, reprint of 1914 ed.), pp. 81,222; William M. Ramsay, *Luke the Physician and Other Studies in the History of Religion* (London: Hodder and Stoughton, 1908), pp. 177-179, 222.

Chapter 5—Legal Testimony About the Resurrection

1. See W. Bauer, *A Greek-English Lexicon of the New Testament and Other Early Christian Literature*, tr. and adap. W.F. Arndt and F.W. Gingrich (Chicago: Univ. of Chicago, 1957), p. 815; J. Thayer, *Thayer's Greek-English Lexicon of the New Testament* (Grand Rapids, MI: Baker, 1982), p. 617; J.H. Moulton and G. Milligan, *The Vocabulary of the Greek Testament Illustrated from the Papyri and Other Non-Literary Sources* (Grand Rapids, MI: Eerdmans, 1930), p. 628; Spiros Zodhiates, *The Hebrew-Greek Key Study Bible* (Grand Rapids, MI: Baker, 1985), p. 71; Kurt Aland et al., *The Greek New Testament* (New York: American Bible Society, 1968), p. 179.

2. Excerpted from The Simon Greenleaf School of Law 1989–1990 catalogue, p. 13.

3. Simon Greenleaf catalogue, pp. 13-26.

4. From personal conversations, March 26 through April 3, 1990, and January 10, 1995.

5. William Lane Craig, *The Son Rises* (Chicago, Moody, 1981), pp. 45-46.

6. As cited in Michael Green, *Man Alive* (Downers Grove, IL: InterVarsity Press, 1969), p. 54.

7. "Hugo Grotius," *Encyclopedia Britannica Micropedia*, vol. 4, p. 753.

8. J.N.D. Anderson, *Christianity: The Witness of History* (London: Tyndale, 1970), pp. 90-105.

9. As cited in Clifford, *Leading Lawyers Look at the Resurrection* (Claremont, IL: Albatross, 1991), p. 112. See also Lionel Luckhoo, *What is Your Verdict?* (Fellowship, 1984).

10. As cited in Clifford, p. 126.

11. Irwin H. Linton, *A Lawyer Examines the Bible* (San Diego: Creation Life, 1977), pp. 13, 196, 192, 50.

12. Linton, pp. 16-17.

13. Linton, p. 16.

14. Wilbur M. Smith, *Therefore Stand* (Grand Rapids, MI: Baker, 1972), p. 423.

15. Josh McDowell, *More Than a Carpenter* (Wheaton, IL: Tyndale, 1983), p. 97.

16. As cited in John Warwick Montgomery, *The Law above the Law* (Minneapolis: Bethany, 1975), pp. 132-133; see also Simon Greenleaf, *The Testimony of the Evangelists* (Grand Rapids, MI: Baker, 1965 repr.), pp. 1-54.

17. From personal conversations, March 26 through April 3, 1990.

18. From personal conversations, March 26 through April 3, 1990.

19. From personal conversation, January 10, 1995 (*Ankerberg Theological Research Institute* news magazine, April 1995, Chattanooga, TN), p. 5.

20. Consider, for example, the memberships of the Victoria Institute of Great Britain, the Christian Medical Society, the Creation Research Society, the American Scientific Affiliation, the Christian Philosophical Society, the Evangelical Theological Society, and other related professional organizations.

21. Pinchas Lapide, tr. William C. Linss, *The Resurrection of Jesus: A Jewish Perspective* (Minneapolis: Augsburg, 1983), pp. 128, 92.

22. Lapide, pp. 126, 131.

23. Lapide, pp. 144, 149.

24. John Warwick Montgomery, "The Quest for Absolutes: Historical Perspectives," class handout (Anaheim, CA: The Simon Greenleaf School of Law, September 1985), p. 7, emphasis in original.

25. S. Sandmel, *Judaism and Christian Beginnings* (New York: Oxford, 1978), p. 397.

26. *The International Standard Bible Encyclopedia*, 1st ed., p. 2566.

27. Clark Pinnock, *Set Forth Your Case: An Examination of Christianity's Credentials* (Chicago: Moody, 1971), pp. 92, 99.

28. Michael Murphy, "The Two-Sided Game of Christian Faith," in *Christianity for the Tough Minded*, ed. John Warwick Montgomery (Minneapolis: Bethany, 1973), p. 255.

29. Green, p. 55.

30. Benjamin B. Warfield, *Selected Shorter Writings*, vol. 1, ed. J.E. Meeter (Phillipsburg, PA: Presbyterian & Reformed, 1980), pp. 178-179, 191.

31. Malcolm Muggeridge, *Jesus: The Man Who Lives* (San Francisco: HarperSanFrancisco, 1976), p. 19.

Chapter 6—Conflicts in the Descriptions of Jesus' Death?

1. L. Morris, *The Gospel According to John*, The New International Commentary on the New Testament (Grand Rapids, MI: Eerdmans, 1973), p. 804.

2. Hugh J. Schonfield, *The Passover Plot* (Boston: Element Books, 1996), p. 163.

3. John K. Naland, "The First Easter: The Evidence for the Resurrection Evaluated," *Free Inquiry*, Spring 1988, p. 12.

4. Michael Green, *The Empty Cross of Jesus* (Downers Grove, IL: InterVarsity Press, 1984), p. 99.

5. John Wenham, *The Easter Enigma* (Grand Rapids, MI: Zondervan, 1984), p. 74.

Chapter 7—Confusion over the First Visitors to the Tomb?

1. John Wenham, *The Easter Enigma* (Grand Rapids, MI: Zondervan, 1984), pp. 69, 39.

2. John Lilly, "Alleged Discrepancies in the Gospel Accounts of the Resurrection," *Catholic Biblical Quarterly* 2 (1940), pp. 105-106.

3. Gleason L. Archer, *Encyclopedia of Bible Difficulties* (Grand Rapids, MI: Zondervan, 1982), pp. 347-348.

4. Lilly, pp. 106-107.

5. Wenham, pp. 81-82.

6. Lilly, p. 103.

Chapter 8—Doubts About the Angels at the Tomb?

1. John Wenham, *The Easter Enigma*, (Grand Rapids, MI: Zondervan, 1984), p. 87, emphasis in original.

2. Wenham, p. 78.

3. Alfred Plummer, as cited in John Lilly, "Alleged Discrepancies in the Gospel Accounts of the Resurrection," *Catholic Biblical Quarterly* 2 (1940), pp. 107-108.

4. Wenham, pp. 85-87.

5. Papias, *Exegesis of the Lord's Oracles* (c. AD 140), as cited in Eusebius, *Ecclesiastical History*, 3.39.15.

6. Wenham, p. 88.

Chapter 9—Clashes in the Accounts of Jesus' Appearances?

1. This and list below adapted from Michael Green, *The Empty Cross of Jesus* (Downers Grove, IL: InterVarsity Press, 1984), p. 114.

2. John Lilly, "Alleged Discrepancies in the Gospel Accounts of the Resurrection," *Catholic Biblical Quarterly* 2 (1940), 109-111.

3. Lilly, p. 111.

4. John K. Naland, "The First Easter: The Evidence for the Resurrection Evaluated," *Free Inquiry,* Spring 1988, p. 16.

5. Hugh J. Schonfield, *The Passover Plot* (Boston: Element Books, 1996), p. 171.

6. Norval Geldenhuys, *Commentary on the Gospel of Luke* (Grand Rapids, MI: Eerdmans, 1975), pp. 627-628.

7. Geldenhuys, pp. 626-627.

Appendix A: The Uniqueness of Christianity and Its Empty Tomb

1. Michael Green, *The Empty Cross of Jesus* (Downers Grove, IL: InterVarsity Press, 1984), p. 92.

2. J.N.D. Anderson, *Christianity and Comparative Religion* (Downers Grove, IL: InterVarsity Press, 1971), p. 51.

3. R.M. Cheyne Edgar, *The Gospel of a Risen Savior* (Edinburgh, 1892), p. 32; as cited in Josh McDowell, *Evidence That Demands a Verdict* (San Bernardino, CA: Here's Life Publishers, 1979), p. 189.

4. Wilbur Smith, *A Great Certainty in This Hour of World Crisis* (Wheaton, IL: Van Kampen Press, 1951), pp. 10-11; as cited in McDowell, *Evidence That Demands a Verdict*, p. 190.

5. Robert Speer, *The Finality of Jesus Christ* (Grand Rapids, MI: Zondervan, 1968), p. 254.

6. Green, pp. 128-130.

7. Merrill Tenney, *The Reality of the Resurrection* (Chicago: Moody Press, 1972), p. 24.

8. Wilbur M. Smith, *Therefore Stand* (Grand Rapids, MI: Baker, 1972), p. 418.

9. Tenney, p. 24.

10. Smith, *Therefore Stand*, p. 417.

11. Plato, *Phaedo* 66, 67, 80; as cited in Calvin Staud; as cited in Smith, *Therefore Stand*, p. 418.

12. Tenney, p. 46.

13. Tenney, p. 24.

14. See James I. Packer, *God's Words* (Downers Grove, IL: InterVarsity Press, 1981).

15. As cited in McDowell, p. 338.

16. See Francis Schaeffer, *He Is There and He Is Not Silent* (Wheaton, IL: Tyndale, 2001); Eugene N. Klaaren, *Religious Origins of Modern Science* (Grand Rapids, MI: Eerdmans, 1977); R. Hooykas, *Religion and the Rise of Modern Science* (Grand Rapids, MI: Eerdmans, 1978); *The Rebirth of America* (Arthur S. DeMoss Foundation, 1986); *The John Ankerberg Show,* "The Founding Fathers" (Chattanooga, TN: 1992).

17. *The World's Great Religions* (New York: Time Inc., 1957), p. 166.

Appendix B: Theories That Deny the Resurrection

1. Wilbur F. Smith, *The Supernaturalness of Christ* (Grand Rapids, MI: Baker, 1974), p. 220.

2. For more thorough descriptions and criticisms of these positions, see Frank Morison, *Who Moved the Stone?* (Downers Grove, IL: InterVarsity Press, 1969), pp. 88-103; Wilbur F. Smith, *Therefore Stand* (Grand Rapids, MI:

Baker, 1972), pp. 359-437; George Eldon Ladd, *I Believe in the Resurrection of Jesus* (Grand Rapids, MI: Eerdmans, 1975), pp. 132-142; Josh McDowell, *Evidence that Demands a Verdict*, vol. 1, 2nd ed. (San Bernardino, CA: Here's Life Publishers, 1979), pp. 232-259; William Lane Craig, *The Son Rises* (Chicago: Moody, 1981), pp. 23-44.

3. See Hugh J. Schonfield, *The Passover Plot* (Boston: Element Books, 1996).

4. Gary Habermas, *Ancient Evidence for the Life of Jesus: Historical Records of His Death and Resurrection* (New York: Nelson, 1984), pp. 20-21.

Appendix C: The Resurrection of Christ and the Mystery Religions

1. See, for example, the review at Tektonics.org. For a further instance, Brown writes, "The vestiges of pagan religion in Christian symbology are undeniable," and, "The pre-Christian God Mithras—called the Son of God and the Light of the World—was born on December 25, died, was buried in a rock tomb, and then resurrected in three days." But anyone who might care to study Mithraism or the alleged influence of paganism on biblical Christianity will prove that Mr. Brown's thesis is "little more than nonsense," in the words of a *New York Times* review ("The DaVinci Con," *New York Times*, February 2, 2004).

2. See "Mystery Religions," *Encyclopedia Britannica Macropedia*, 15th ed. This material is adapted from the authors' *The Secret Teachings of the Masonic Lodge: A Christian Perspective* (Chicago: Moody Press, 1991), pp. 244-245.

3. See Jack Finegan, *Myth and Mystery: An Introduction to the Pagan Religions of the Biblical World* (Grand Rapids, MI: Baker, 1989).

4. Edward Evans-Pritchard, *Theories of Primitive Religion* (1965), p. 42; as cited in Tom Snyder, *Myth Conceptions* (Grand Rapids, MI: Baker Books, 1995), p. 191.

5. Samuel N. Kramer, *Mythologies of the Ancient World* (Garden City, NY: Doubleday, 1961), p. 10; as cited in Josh McDowell, *Evidence That Demands a Verdict* (San Bernardino, CA: Campus Crusade for Christ, 1972), p. 263.

6. Pierre Lambrechts, "La Resurrection de Adonis," in *Mélanges Isidore Levy* (1955), pp. 207-240; as cited in Edwin Yamauchi, "The Passover Plot or Easter Triumph?" in John Warwick Montgomery, ed., *Christianity for the Tough Minded* (Minneapolis: Bethany, 1973).

7. Lambrechts.

8. "Adonis," *Encyclopedia Britannica Macropedia*, vol. 15 (1969).

9. As cited in Wilbur M. Smith, *Therefore Stand* (New Canaan, CT: Keats, 1981), p. 583.

10. André Boulanger, as cited in Smith, p. 583.

11. C.S. Lewis, *Miracles: A Preliminary Study* (London: Collins/Fontana, 1970), p. 119.

12. Lewis, p. 118.

13. As cited in Snyder, p. 194.

14. J.N.D. Anderson, *Christianity and Comparative Religion* (Downers Grove, IL: InterVarsity Press, 1977), p. 22.

15. "Mystery Religions," *Encyclopedia Britannica Macropedia*, 15th ed. (1969).

16. Ronald H. Nash, *Christianity and the Hellenistic World* (Grand Rapids, MI: Zondervan/Probe, 1984), pp. 171-172.

17. Nash, p. 173.

18. Nash, pp. 192-199; citing Metzger on the cult of Cybele.

LIST OF SOURCES AND SUGGESTED READING

Anderson, J.N.D. *Christianity: The Witness of History.* London: Tyndale, 1970.

Babcock, J.F. "The Resurrection—A Credibility Gap." In *Christianity for the Tough Minded,* ed. John Warwick Montgomery. Minneapolis: Bethany, 1973.

Barbet, Pierre. *A Doctor at Calvary.* Garden City, NY: Doubleday, 1963.

Bartlett, C. *As a Lawyer Sees Jesus: A Logical Analysis of the Scriptural and Historical Record.* Cincinnati, OH: New Life, 1960.

Brown, Colin. *Miracles and the Critical Mind.* Grand Rapids, MI: Eerdmans, 1984.

Bruce, F.F. *The New Testament Documents: Are They Reliable?* 5th ed. Downers Grove, IL: InterVarsity Press, 1971.

Clifford, R. *Leading Lawyers Look at the Resurrection.* Claremont, CA: Albatross, 1991.

Craig, William Lane. *The Son Rises: Historical Evidence for the Resurrection of Jesus.* Chicago: Moody, 1981.

Foreman, D. *Crucify Him: A Lawyer Looks at the Trial of Jesus.* Grand Rapids, MI: Zondervan, 1990.

Geisler, Norman L. *The Battle for the Resurrection.* Nashville, TN: Thomas Nelson, 1984.

Green, Michael. *Man Alive!* Downers Grove, IL: InterVarsity Press, 1969.

———. *The Empty Cross of Jesus.* Downers Grove, IL: InterVarsity Press, 1984.

Grieve, V. *Your Verdict on the Empty Tomb of Jesus.* Downers Grove, IL: InterVarsity Press, 1988.

Habermas, Gary. *Ancient Evidence for the Life of Jesus: Historical Records of His Death and Resurrection.* New York: Nelson, 1984.

Hanson, G. *The Resurrection and the Life.* New York: Revell, 1911.

Ladd, George Eldon. *I Believe in the Resurrection of Jesus.* Grand Rapids, MI: Eerdmans, 1975.

Lapide, Pinchas, tr. William C. Linss. *The Resurrection of Jesus: A Jewish Perspective,* reprint ed. Eugene, OR: Wipf & Stock Publishers, 2002.

Lewis, C.S. *Mere Christianity.* New York: Macmillan, 1952.

————. *Miracles.* London: Fontana, 1970.

Lilly, John. "Alleged Discrepancies in the Gospel Accounts of the Resurrection." *Catholic Biblical Quarterly* 2 (1940).

Linton, Irwin H. *A Lawyer Examines the Bible: A Defense of the Christian Faith.* San Diego: Creation Life, 1977.

McDowell, Josh. *Evidence that Demands a Verdict,* 2 vols., 2nd ed. San Bernardino, CA: Here's Life Publishers, 1979.

————. *More Than a Carpenter.* Wheaton: Tyndale, 1983.

Miethe, T.L., ed. *Did Jesus Rise from the Dead? The Resurrection Debate.* New York: Harper & Row, 1987.

Montgomery, John Warwick. *Evidence for Faith.* Richardson, TX: Probe Books, 1991.

————. *History and Christianity.* San Bernardino, CA: Here's Life Publishers, 1983.

————, ed. *Jurisprudence: A Book of Readings.* Deerfield, IL: International Scholarly Publishers, 1974.

————. *The Law Above the Law.* Minneapolis: Bethany, 1975.

Morison, Frank. *Who Moved the Stone?* Downers Grove, IL: InterVarsity Press, 1969.

Morris, Henry. *Many Infallible Proofs.* San Diego: Master, 1982.

Murphy, Michael. "The Two-Sided Game of Christian Faith." In *Christianity for the Tough Minded,* ed. John Warwick Montgomery. Minneapolis: Bethany, 1973.

Newman, R.C. "Miracles and the Historicity of the Easter Week Narratives." In *Evidence for Faith,* John Warwick Montgomery, ed. Dallas: Probe, 1991.

Orr, J. *The Resurrection of Jesus.* Joplin, MO: College, 1972 repr.

Pinnock, Clark. *Set Forth Your Case: An Examination of Christianity's Credentials.* Chicago: Moody, 1971.

Ramm, Bernard. *Protestant Christian Evidences.* Chicago: Moody, 1971.

Reicke, B. *The Roots of the Synoptic Gospels.* Philadelphia: Fortress, 1986.

Robinson, J.A.T. *Redating the New Testament.* Philadelphia: Westminster, 1976.

Smith, Wilbur M. *The Supernaturalness of Christ.* Grand Rapids, MI: Baker, 1974.

————. *Therefore Stand.* Grand Rapids, MI: Baker, 1972.

Sparrow-Simpson, W.J. *The Resurrection and Modern Thought.* London: Longmans, 1911.

Stott, John R.W. *Basic Christianity.* Downers Grove, IL: InterVarsity Press, 1971.

Strobel, Lee. *The Case for Easter.* Grand Rapids, MI: Zondervan, 2004.

Tenney, Merrill. *The Reality of the Resurrection.* Chicago: Moody, 1972.

Thompson, E.S. *On the Physical Cause of the Death of Christ.* London: SPCK, 1984.

Torrey, R.A. "The Certainty and Importance of the Bodily Resurrection of Jesus Christ from the Dead," rev. and ed. G.B. Stanton. In *The Fundamentals for Today,* ed. C.L. Feinberg. Grand Rapids, MI: Kregel, 1964.

Webster, W. "The Credibility of the Resurrection of Christ upon the Testimony of the Apostles." *The Simon Greenleaf Law Review* 6 (1986-87), pp. 99-145.

Wenham, John. *The Easter Enigma.* Grand Rapids, MI: Zondervan, 1984.

———. *Redating Matthew, Mark and Luke: A Fresh Assault on the Synoptic Problem.* Downers Grove, IL: InterVarsity Press, 1992.

Westcott, B.F. *The Gospel of the Resurrection,* 4th ed. London: Macmillan, 1879.

Wilson, C. *The False Trials of Jesus Christ.* Oklahoma City: Hearthstone, 1990.

Fast Facts® Books from Harvest House

FAST FACTS® ON FALSE TEACHING
by *Ron Carlson & Ed Decker*

Two cult experts combine their extensive knowledge to give you quick, clear facts about 16 major false teachings of today, and others. Short, informative chapters highlight major issues and contrast false teachings with the truth of God's revealed Word. An easy-to-use resource that gives you powerful insights for sharing the gospel.

FAST FACTS® ON ISLAM
by *John Ankerberg & John Weldon*

Ankerberg and Weldon's Q-and-A format explains Islam's beginnings, Muslims' beliefs about God and Jesus, and how Islamic beliefs relate to recent terrorist acts. A must-have for Christ-centered insight into a growing religious and political power.

FAST FACTS® ON JEHOVAH'S WITNESSES
by *John Ankerberg & John Weldon*

From blood transfusions to works salvation, Ankerberg and Weldon expose the unorthodox doctrines and unbiblical teachings of Jehovah's Witnesses. Whether you're looking for specific information or an overall understanding, you'll find this guide extremely helpful.

FAST FACTS® ON THE MIDDLE EAST CONFLICT
by *J. Randall Price*

Price provides "insider" information to answer critical questions regarding the current controversies and viewpoints in the Middle East. You'll discover a fascinating timeline of the conflict, a close look at the groups involved, possible scenarios for Jerusalem's future, and handy maps, charts, and quick-reference sidebars packed with solid, factual information.

FAST FACTS® ON MORMONISM
by *John Ankerberg & John Weldon*

Was God ever a man? Were Jesus and Lucifer brothers? From Mormon definitions of traditional Christian terms to their view of the Bible, Ankerberg and Weldon explore the fundamentals of Mormonism and how they compare to orthodox Christianity.

FAST FACTS® ON ROMAN CATHOLICISM
by *John Ankerberg & John Weldon*

Covering the Pope's role in the church, Mary's exaltation, and the authority of Catholic Tradition, this book delves into Roman Catholicism to reveal its beliefs and practices and how they compare to God's Word.

FAST FACTS® ON THE MASONIC LODGE
by *John Ankerberg & John Weldon*

Find out whether Masonry and Christianity are truly compatible. The authors clarify Masons' claims and terminology, asking: Is Freemasonry a religion? What do Masonic symbols represent? What do Masons teach about Jesus and the God of the Bible? A great resource if you're a Mason who's unsure about the Lodge's teaching, if you're a friend or relative of a Mason, or if you simply want to be informed about this influential organization.

HARVEST HOUSE
PUBLISHERS

HARVEST HOUSE BOOKS BY
JOHN ANKERBERG AND JOHN WELDON

Creation vs. Evolution: What You Need to Know

Fast Facts® on Islam

Fast Facts® on Jehovah's Witnesses

Fast Facts® on Mormonism

Fast Facts® on Roman Catholicism

Fast Facts® on the Masonic Lodge

The Passion and the Empty Tomb

What Do Mormons Really Believe?

The "Facts On" Series

The Facts on Angels

The Facts on Halloween

The Facts on Homosexuality

The Facts on Islam

The Facts on Jehovah's Witnesses

The Facts on Roman Catholicism

The Facts on the King James Only Debate

The Facts on the Masonic Lodge

The Facts on the Mormon Church

The Facts on Why You Can Believe the Bible

The Facts on World Religions